THE CONSTITUTION OF

THE UNITED STATES

DAVID P. CURRIE

The CONSTITUTION *of the* UNITED STATES

A Primer for the People

SECOND EDITION

THE UNIVERSITY OF CHICAGO PRESS

Chicago and London

The University of Chicago Press, Chicago 60637
The University of Chicago Press, Ltd., London
© 1988, 2000 by The University of Chicago
All rights reserved. Published 2000
Printed in the United States of America

09 08 07 06 05 04   3 4 5

ISBN: 0-226-13104-1 (paper)

Library of Congress Cataloging-in-Publication Data

Currie, David P.
   The Constitution of the United States: a primer for the people / David
P. Currie.—2nd ed.
      p. cm.
   Includes bibliographical references and index.
   ISBN: 0-226-13103-3 (cloth : alk. paper) — ISBN: 0-226-13104-1
(pbk. : alk. paper)
   1. Constitutional law—United States.   I. Title.
   KF4550.Z9 C88 2000
   342.73'02—dc21   99-055538

CONTENTS

PREFACE

The Constitution of the United States is over two hundred years old. It was a remarkable document when drafted in 1787, and it has survived remarkably well. With a few major changes it has continued to provide an exemplary framework for representative government and admirable protection for fundamental rights.

Everyone admires the Constitution; few understand it. The document itself can be read in a few minutes, and every citizen should read it. Yet to read the Constitution alone is not to know what it means, for some of its most important provisions are quite imprecise.

We all know from news reports that the Constitution has something to say about affirmative action, abortion, and school prayers, but you will find none of these terms in the Constitution. What you will find are provisions forbidding state or federal governments to deny "equal protection of the laws," deprive persons of life, liberty, or property without "due process of law," or make laws respecting "an establishment of religion." The men who drafted the Constitution knew that if it was to last it must speak in broad and general terms, leaving details to be worked out by interpretation as the "great outlines" of the Constitution were applied to a myriad of unforeseeable problems.[1]

Thus the Constitution can be understood only by examining how it has been interpreted and applied in the years since its adoption. Every government official—legislative, executive, or judicial—must interpret the Constitution in order to determine the limits of his or her authority. Moreover, the judges have construed the Constitution to give them power to determine the constitutionality of legislative and executive acts in the course of deciding lawsuits, and consequently their decisions have assumed special importance in establishing what the Constitution means.

The purpose of this book is to introduce the interested citizen to the Constitution as it actually operates, in light of the decisions of the courts that interpret and apply it. No knowledge of law is required to understand the Constitution, but a knowledge of the decisions is, and I aim to provide it.

The Supreme Court has done an admirable job in exercising its awesome responsibility to interpret the Constitution. Like all human institutions, it has also made mistakes, and I shall try to point some of them out. This is an opinionated book, and needless to say other observers have other opinions. I can only hope that I have presented both sides of any disputed question fairly enough that the reader can come to his or her own conclusion.

Let me state some of my underlying premises. As it says, the Constitution is "the supreme law of the land," and all government officers must swear to respect it (art. VI). This means that neither judges nor other officials have the right to ignore constitutional provisions with which they disagree. Conversely, judges have no more right to invent limitations on governmental action not found in the Constitution than to disregard those the framers put there. For the same clause that makes the Constitution the "law of the land" gives identical status to federal statutes enacted "in pursuance thereof," while the Tenth Amendment reserves to the states all powers not taken from them by the Constitution.

This is not to say that either the text of the Constitution or the limited evidence we have of the framers' intentions answers every question of constitutional interpretation. It is not to pretend that the framers either thought out all the ramifications of their terminology or would have agreed in all respects if they had. Nor is it to deny the possibility that a particular provision may have been meant to leave considerable latitude to the interpreter's judgment. A ban on "exces-

sive fines," for example, is obviously less confining than a requirement
that the President "have . . . attained the age of thirty-five years." The
point is only that it is inappropriate for any government official to
substitute his or her judgment for that of the "people of the United
States" in any case in which the latter can fairly be ascertained.

The official's task, in other words, is to follow the Constitution.
To do so he or she must first determine what it means, and to do that
one must examine its words, its history, and its purposes. "Perhaps the
safest rule of interpretation," wrote the great Justice Joseph Story in
1842, "will be found to be to look to the nature and objects of the particular powers, duties and rights, with all the lights and aids of con-
temporary history; and to give to the words of each just such operation and force, consistent with their legitimate meaning, as may fairly
secure and attain the ends proposed."[2]

The critical tone of some of my observations should not be taken
to indicate a lack of admiration either for the Constitution or for
those who have struggled in good faith with the challenging task of
implementing its open-ended provisions. This book is offered in the
conviction that the Constitution deserves to be better understood by
those fortunate enough to live under it, and in the hope that greater
appreciation of its provisions may help to assure that it will long continue, in the words of its Preamble, "to secure the blessings of liberty
to ourselves and our posterity."

One final word: There are footnotes. You needn't read them. They
are there to provide citations, explanations, and tangential information without interrupting or lengthening the text. I have put them at
the back to keep them out of your way; the flesh is weak.

I am grateful to Gerhard Casper, Barbara Flynn Currie, Patricia
M. Evans, Philip B. Kurland, Geoffrey R. Stone, and Hans Zeisel for
their generous advice and encouragement with respect to the first edition of this book, which appeared in 1987. The present edition in-
corporates developments since that time.

1   *Introduction*

DISENCHANTED with British rule, thirteen American colonies sent delegates to the Continental Congress in Philadelphia in 1776. There they adopted the Declaration of Independence, which was confirmed after the Revolution by the Treaty of Paris in 1783. The colonies had become independent states.

They had also established a confederation. Shortly after declaring independence, the Continental Congress had proposed the Articles of Confederation, and by 1781 all thirteen states had ratified them. These Articles were the first constitution of the United States.[1]

The confederation created by the articles was quite feeble. The central government did have broad powers over military and foreign affairs. In domestic matters, however, except for the coining and regulation of money, nearly all authority was reserved to the individual states. There was no independent executive authority, and there were essentially no federal courts. Congress lacked power even to impose taxes to cover federal expenditures. The central government was dependent upon the states.

Dissatisfaction with the Articles of Confederation prompted the states in 1787 to send delegates to Philadelphia once again, in hopes of strengthening the central government. Though authorized only to propose amendments to the articles, the convention resolved to scrap them entirely and propose a brand new Constitution. Moreover, invoking the principle of popular sovereignty embodied in the Declaration of Independence, the delegates decided to disregard a provision in the articles requiring the consent of all thirteen state legislatures before they could be altered. "We must go to the original powers of Society," James Wilson argued; "the House on fire must be extinguished, without a scrupulous regard to ordinary rights."[2] Within two years, after ratification by conventions in nine states as provided in its seventh Article, the new Constitution went into effect.

This Constitution has been amended from time to time, but its basic provisions are still in force. It consists of seven articles and twenty-six (or twenty-seven) amendments.[3] It grants powers to the central government, divides those powers among the various branches, and limits the powers of both the central government and the states.

The government the Constitution established was in the main a free and representative one, though marred by provisions recognizing the existence of slavery.[4] It was also a limited one, for despite their perception of the need for additional federal authority the framers were distrustful of government in general and of the central government in particular. Among the most prominent characteristics of the Constitution, therefore, are three great structural principles designed to guard against the possible abuse of governmental power.

The principle of *federalism* limits the risk of official oppression by dividing power between the nation and its constituent states; that of *separation of powers* does so by allocating authority among the three branches of the federal government. The principle of *checks and balances* provides further protection by giving one branch authority to impede misguided or illegal actions of another. None of these three principles is mentioned by name in the Constitution, but each is reflected in a number of its express provisions.

CONGRESS

Article I, § 1 entrusts federal legislative authority to the United States Congress, which is composed of two chambers—the Senate and the House of Representatives. Members of the House are elected directly by the people for two-year terms, and the seats are distributed among the states according to population (art. I, § 2). California thus has more than fifty representatives; Delaware and Alaska have only one.

In the Senate, on the other hand, each state has two members (art. I, § 3), and under article V this provision effectively cannot be amended.[5] These concessions to the smaller states were the price of their approval of the Constitution.

Originally Senators were elected by the state legislatures, permitting the states themselves to play a role in the national government. The Seventeenth Amendment altered this procedure in the interest of democracy; since 1913 Senators too have been directly elected by the people.

Article I imposes minimal age, citizenship, and residence requirements for both Senators and Representatives.[6] Neither Congress nor the states may add to these qualifications. As the Supreme Court said in striking down term limits for members of Congress in 1995, the constitutional list is exclusive; beyond the most fundamental restrictions, the framers meant to give voters maximum freedom to elect whomever they chose.[7]

Most of the subjects of possible federal legislation are listed in article I, § 8. Congress may raise and support armies and navies and declare war. It may regulate commerce with foreign nations, among the states, and with Indian tribes. It may coin money and make rules for the naturalization of foreigners. It may enact patent, copyright, and bankruptcy laws, establish post offices, and govern the District of Columbia. It may impose taxes and borrow money to pay federal obligations. Finally, it may enact all laws "necessary and proper" to the execution of any powers entrusted to the central government.

Other provisions give Congress miscellaneous additional powers. Article IV authorizes it to admit new states, govern federal territories, and prescribe the effect of one state's laws and decisions in the courts of another. article V empowers Congress to propose constitutional amendments. Amendments 13–15, 19, 23–24, and 26 authorize Congress to enforce their provisions "by appropriate legislation."

On their face these powers do not seem very extensive. Apart from relatively minor or incidental matters, the Constitution added to the authority already conferred by the articles of Confederation only the powers to tax and to regulate commerce. Even this limited authority, moreover, is further restricted by article I, § 9, which among other things forbids Congress to tax exports or to prefer one state's ports over another and requires that "direct" taxes be apportioned among the states according to population. This last restriction effectively prevented federal income taxes until the Sixteenth Amendment was adopted in 1913.[8]

The enumeration of congressional powers implies that Congress has *only* the authority given it by the Constitution, and the Tenth Amendment confirms this conclusion: "The powers not delegated to the United States by the Constitution, and not prohibited by it to the States, are reserved to the States respectively, or to the people." Through the process of interpretation, however, the modest provisions just described have been held to give Congress surprisingly broad legislative authority.

Like the Constitution itself, statutes lawfully enacted by Congress are "the supreme law of the land" (art. VI). Thus if federal and state law conflict, the former prevails.

THE PRESIDENT

Article II, § 1 entrusts federal executive power to the President of the United States, who is elected for four years and (since adoption of the Twenty-second Amendment in 1951) no more than twice. Because the authors of the Constitution did not trust the people to make a wise choice, the President is elected not directly but by "electors" chosen by the voters of the several states (art. II, § 1; and amend. 12). This system never worked as the framers intended; from almost the outset, electors have been mere figureheads who rubber-stamp the voters' choice.

Each state elects a number of electors corresponding to the total of its Senators and Representatives, and since 1961 the District of

Columbia (which has no vote in Congress) chooses no more "than the least populous state" (amend. 23). Since each state has two Senators regardless of population, the smaller states are somewhat over-represented in the choice of a President as well. Moreover, state laws generally provide that the winner of the popular vote within a state receives *all* of its electoral votes. These factors make it possible for a candidate who receives a majority of the total popular vote to lose the election. This actually occurred when Rutherford B. Hayes defeated Samuel Tilden in 1876.

If no candidate receives a majority of the electoral votes, the House of Representatives selects the President "from the persons having the highest numbers not exceeding three."[9] In this process each state has only one vote regardless of its number of Representatives, and a majority of all states is required (amend. 12).

Originally the candidate finishing second in the presidential balloting became Vice-President. After the unexpected tie vote between Thomas Jefferson and his running mate Aaron Burr in 1800, however, the Twelfth Amendment required the electors to vote separately for the two offices.

The Vice-President's principal function is to assume the duties of a President who dies or becomes incapable of carrying out his duties (art. II, § 1; amend. 25). The Vice-President also "act[s] as President" if (through inability of any candidate to obtain a majority in either the Electoral College or the House) no President has been selected (amend. 20).

So long as there is a competent President, the Constitution gives the Vice-President little to do beyond the largely mechanical task of presiding over the Senate—with the occasionally significant prerogative of voting to break a tie (art. I, § 3). This substantial lack of duties was the basis of the waggish inquiry, "whatever became of Hubert?"—the respected and influential Senator Hubert Humphrey, who became Vice-President in 1965—and disappeared.

The President's independence from Congress is strengthened by the fact that he (or she) can be removed only by the difficult process of impeachment. A majority vote of the House of Representatives is required to bring charges against the President, and a two-thirds vote of the Senate is required for removal (art. I, §§ 2, 3).[10] Like other federal officers, a President may not be removed for political reasons, but only for "treason, bribery, or other high crimes and misdemeanors"—an imprecise concept that basically requires a serious abuse of official power.[11]

No President has actually been removed from office by this procedure. After the Civil War an essentially political attempt to remove Andrew Johnson failed by a single vote in the Senate. In 1974, in what was widely regarded as a vindication of the impeachment provisions, Richard Nixon resigned after the House Judiciary Committee voted to charge him with concealing information about the burglary of a Democratic campaign office, discriminatory enforcement of federal laws against political opponents, and disobedience of a subpoena issued by the committee itself. President Clinton was impeached in 1998 for perjury and obstruction of justice in connection with the Monica Lewinsky scandal, but the Senate failed to convict him.

The independence of members of Congress from the executive and judicial branches is reinforced by the provision of article I, § 6 that "for any speech or debate in either House, they shall not be questioned in any other place." There is no comparable provision expressly protecting the President from outside interference, but the Supreme Court has found such protection implicit in article II's provisions for an independent executive. The confidentiality of executive communications is guarded by a conditional "executive privilege" that can be overridden by important countervailing interests;[12] to avoid deterring the President from performing his duties, he may not be sued for damages arising out of his official actions.[13]

Clinton v. Jones, decided in 1997, refused to extend these precedents to permit a President to defer a damage suit unrelated to his duties until he was out of office.[14] President Jefferson had powerfully stated the argument for immunity in resisting the suggestion that he could be ordered to give evidence in person in the treason trial of Aaron Burr. There might be many such demands, he said, on a President's time; "[t]o comply with such calls would leave the nation without an executive branch, whose agency is understood to be so constantly necessary that it is the sole branch which the constitution requires to be always in function. It could not, then, intend that it should be withdrawn from its station by any co-ordinate authority."[15]

Jefferson provided the court with the documentary evidence it demanded, but Chief Justice Marshall did not insist on his presence at the trial. Indeed he essentially conceded the correctness of Jefferson's position: If attendance in court would significantly interfere with the President's duties, he had only to say so and he would be excused.[16]

The accommodating language that Marshall employed in acknowledging that the President's schedule might justify relieving him from the relatively trivial inconvenience of appearing at someone else's trial contrasts sharply with the lack of concern displayed by a unanimous Supreme Court in *Clinton* over subjecting one of his successors to the continuing burden of defending a personal tort action that endangered both his reputation and his fortune. Arguably the President should be put to the task of asserting, or more doubtfully of convincing the court, that the demands of the office preclude his devoting the requisite attention to the individual proceeding;[17] but surely Jefferson and Marshall were right that there must be some means of ensuring that the President is not distracted from doing his job.

Most of the President's powers are enumerated in article II, §§ 2, 3. He is commander in chief of the armed forces. He has authority to pardon federal crimes, except in cases of impeachment. With Senate consent he appoints judges and other federal officers and makes treaties with foreign nations. In other respects as well he plays the leading role in international affairs—partly on the basis of the unprepossessing provision empowering him to "receive ambassadors and other public ministers"[18] and partly on the theory that certain foreign-affairs powers are inherent in the office itself.[19] The further direction that the President "take care that the laws be faithfully executed" gives him basic responsibility for the enforcement of federal law.

Finally, the President plays an important role in the legislative process by virtue of the veto power granted by article I, § 7: If he refuses to approve a bill passed by Congress, it becomes a law only if passed again by a two-thirds majority of each House.[20] He also may, and often does, recommend legislation for congressional consideration (art. II, § 3).

THE COURTS

Article III, § 1 entrusts federal judicial power to the Supreme Court of the United States and such inferior tribunals as Congress chooses to establish. Since 1789 there have been federal trial courts (United States District Courts) in every state, and since 1891 there have also been intermediate Courts of Appeals.

The same section provides that federal judges hold office "during good behavior." Apart from the limited possibility of impeachment, this is understood to mean for life, and a further provision assures that their compensation may not be reduced while they are in office. The purpose of these provisions is to ensure that the judges can do their job without fear of reprisals by other branches.[21]

Like Congress, the federal courts have only the authority granted them by the Constitution. Their most important function is to decide "cases" and "controversies"—that is, lawsuits. Under article II, § 2 Congress may also authorize the courts to appoint "inferior officers" who otherwise would be named by the President with Senate approval. Although the context suggests that this provision was designed to permit courts to appoint their own clerks and other judicial officers,[22] Congress in the wake of the Watergate affair authorized them to appoint special prosecutors as well, and the Supreme Court sustained the provision.[23]

Not all lawsuits may be decided by federal courts; their authority is limited to certain *kinds* of controversies that the framers of the Constitution thought appropriate subjects of national concern.

The most important of these are cases involving the Constitution itself, federal laws, or treaties ("federal-question" cases). Federal authority to decide these disputes helps to ensure the supremacy and uniformity of federal law. Admiralty cases, which generally have to do with shipping, were included because of the international nature of the shipping business and its importance to the new nation.

Federal judicial authority also extends to controversies between citizens of different states ("diversity of citizenship" cases), in order to avoid the risk that a state court might prefer its own citizens in disputes with outsiders. For similar reasons, federal courts may also decide controversies between states and cases to which the United States is a party. The authority of federal courts to entertain suits against states, however, was limited by the Eleventh Amendment in 1795.

The many types of lawsuits not listed in article III—including most contract, property, personal-injury, criminal, and domestic-relations matters—are reserved to the state courts; every state has a set of courts of its own. State courts may also decide most cases that fall within the authority of the federal courts, if the parties so desire. While the Necessary and Proper Clause empowers Congress to make federal-court authority over these cases exclusive, it has not generally done so.

Unless a state or a foreign diplomat is a party, the Supreme Court functions only as a court of last resort ("appellate jurisdiction"). A dispute is first decided by a federal District Court or by a state trial court; the losing party may then appeal the trial court's decision, in some cases ultimately to the Supreme Court of the United States. State-court decisions, however, are subject to Supreme Court review only to the extent they involve the Constitution or other federal law.[24]

The Bill of Rights

Article V provides for amendment of the Constitution. No amendment may deprive a state of its equal voice in the Senate without its consent, but otherwise any provision may be freely amended.[25]

Precisely because the amending power is so broad, the process of amendment was made difficult, in order to prevent ill-considered changes. It normally requires a two-thirds vote of both Houses of Congress to propose a constitutional amendment and the concurrence of three fourths of the states to approve it. This has occurred only twenty-six or twenty-seven times in two hundred years.[26] An alternate provision for a constitutional convention to propose amendments has never been used—partly out of fear that a convention might tamper with the basic fabric of the Constitution.

Although the Constitution gave the federal government only limited powers, widespread fears were expressed in the state ratifying conventions that it might abuse its authority. To allay these concerns, Congress in one of its first acts in 1789 proposed twelve constitutional amendments. Ten of these, including the Bill of Rights, were ratified within two years and became the first ten amendments to the Constitution.[27]

The First Amendment forbids Congress to make laws abridging the freedom of speech, press, assembly, or religion, as well as laws "respecting an establishment of religion." A response to the "established" churches in England and in some of the colonies, this last clause has been interpreted to require a broad separation between church and state.

The Second Amendment, which has been much in the news lately, guarantees "the right of the people to keep and bear arms"—in order, as the text provides, to ensure the availability of a "well-regu-lated militia." Whether in light of this stated purpose the amendment permits *individuals* to possess weapons has been hotly disputed, and the Supreme Court has never resolved the issue.

The Third Amendment protects against the quartering of troops in private homes. The Fourth, in response to the infamous "writs of assistance" employed to enforce oppressive British trade laws before the Revolution, forbids "unreasonable searches and seizures" and pro-vides that search or arrest warrants may be issued only upon "proba-ble cause."

Amendments 5, 6, and 8 deal largely with the rights of persons ac-cused of federal crimes. To protect against government oppression, defendants are entitled to a speedy and public trial before a jury of their fellow citizens. To ensure a fair trial, they are entitled to confront opposing witnesses, to present witnesses of their own, and to have the assistance of counsel. They may not be tried or punished more than once for a single offense, subjected to "cruel and unusual" punish-ments, or compelled to give evidence against themselves.

This last provision is the famous "privilege against self-incrimina-tion," sometimes referred to simply as "the Fifth Amendment," which is often invoked by persons under investigation or on trial for alleged crimes. It rests in part on the perception that it is unjust to place a de-fendant in the "cruel trilemma" of choosing among confession, per-jury, and contempt of court, and it has been defended as a safeguard against the use of torture to elicit confessions.

The Fifth Amendment also forbids the taking of private property for public use without just compensation; if the government wants to build a post office on my land, it must pay for it. The mysterious provision of the same amendment that no one may be deprived of life, liberty, or property "without due process of law" is explored in detail below.

The Seventh Amendment requires a jury trial in certain *civil* cases, which it describes as "suits at common law." These are controversies of the kinds traditionally decided by "common law" rather than "equity" or "admiralty" courts in England—roughly speaking, those in which the only remedy sought is money damages and ships are not involved.[28]

The Ninth Amendment enigmatically provides that the Constitution's "enumeration of certain rights . . . shall not be construed to deny or disparage others retained by the people." The Tenth (already noted) reserves to the states powers not delegated to the United States or prohibited by the Constitution.

LATER AMENDMENTS

As originally adopted, the Constitution contained few limitations on state authority. Article I, § 10 did exclude the states from certain fields entrusted to the federal government, such as money matters and most military or foreign affairs. The same section also forbade the states to pass laws making past conduct criminal ("ex post facto laws"), declaring individuals guilty of crime ("bills of attainder"), or "impairing the obligation of contracts."

The ex post facto and attainder prohibitions were also made applicable to Congress by § 9 of the same article; the Supreme Court invoked them both in striking down requirements that members of certain professions swear that they had not given comfort to the Confederacy during the Civil War.[29] The Contract Clause was of considerable significance during the nineteenth century, when among other things it was held to forbid the revocation of land grants and corporate charters; twentieth-century decisions have so narrowed its scope that it no longer plays an important role.[30]

Article IV imposed additional limitations on the states in the interest of interstate harmony. Citizens of one state were required to be treated as citizens in another. Each state was required to respect the "public acts, records, and judicial proceedings" of other states and to return both fugitive slaves and persons charged elsewhere with crimes. Article VI, as noted, required the states to respect federal law.

Two of the first eight amendments expressly applied only to the federal government. The First speaks only of "Congress," the Seventh of the "court[s] of the United States." Despite their general wording, the others too were adopted in response to fears of federal rather than state authority; and as a result they were held not to limit the powers of the states.[31]

More significant restrictions on state authority were imposed by the "Civil War Amendments" (13–15), which were adopted between 1865 and 1870 in order to combat racial discrimination, and which are discussed in chapters 5 and 6. The Thirteenth Amendment abolished slavery. The Fourteenth, which has proved one of the most significant parts of the Constitution, contains several important provisions. In order to overrule the *Dred Scott* decision, which had held that blacks were not citizens,[32] § 1 declares virtually all persons born or naturalized in the United States "citizens of the United States and of the State wherein they reside."[33] Most important, it also forbids the states to abridge the "privileges or immunities" of United States citizens, to deny anyone within its jurisdiction "the equal protection of the laws," or (as the Fifth Amendment already provided in the case of the federal government) to deprive any person of life, liberty, or property "without due process of law." Among other things, this last provision has been held to make most of the Bill of Rights applicable to individual states. The Fifteenth Amendment forbids the United States as well as the states to deny any citizen the right to vote on grounds of race, and later amendments extend the vote to women and eighteen-year-olds as well (amend. 19, 26). Each of these amendments authorizes Congress to enforce its provisions by appropriate legislation.

The remaining amendments need not detain us long; some have been mentioned already. The Eleventh limited federal-court authority to entertain suits against states; the Twelfth revised the procedure for presidential elections. The Sixteenth removed an obstacle to federal income taxes; the Seventeenth provided for popular election of Senators. The Eighteenth instituted nationwide prohibition of alcoholic beverages, and the Twenty-first abolished it. The Twentieth ("lame duck") Amendment reduced the delay between the election and inauguration of executive and legislative officers; the Twenty-second basically limited Presidents to two terms; the Twenty-third gave District of Columbia citizens the right to choose presidential electors. The Twenty-fourth abolished poll tax requirements in federal elections; the Twenty-fifth provided for transferring responsibility to the Vice-President in case of presidential disability.

So much for the outlines of the Constitution. Let us proceed to a closer examination of what it means.

2   *Judicial Review*

JUDICIAL REVIEW is the power of courts to determine the legality of acts of other branches of government. In the United States it includes the authority, when the issue is presented in a case within the court's jurisdiction, to declare federal and state statutes unconstitutional.

Judicial review in this sense has been fundamental to our constitutional scheme. It is in the exercise of this power, for example, that the Supreme Court has outlawed school segregation, abortion laws, and school prayers. Yet the reader will find no explicit reference in the Constitution to judicial review of federal laws. It was the judges themselves who, guided by the spirit of the Constitution, discovered judicial review in its unclear provisions. This discovery was explained in the famous decision of *Marbury v. Madison* in 1803.[1]

After the election of Thomas Jefferson and of a Congress dominated by his supporters in 1800, the defeated President John Adams had done his best to preserve a portion of his party's power by appointing a number of Federalist judges. Among them was a lowly Justice of the Peace for the District of Columbia named William Marbury, whose duties included such momentous matters as the performance of marriages and the trial of petty offenses.

Marbury's commission had been signed and sealed but not delivered. James Madison, the new Secretary of State, refused to hand it over, and Marbury went directly to the Supreme Court.

Chief Justice John Marshall and his Federalist colleagues made clear that Madison had acted illegally in withholding Marbury's commission. When that document had been signed and sealed, Marbury had become a judge protected by statute against removal. Thus he had a right to the office and to his commission.

Moreover, wrote Marshall, it was the obligation of judges to protect the rights of the individual against infringement by the government. "The very essence of civil liberty," he said, "consists in the right of every individual to claim the protection of the laws, whenever he receives an injury." Although the courts could not interfere with the exercise of discretion confided to the executive, they were entitled to order even Cabinet officers to carry out their legal duties. Congress had recognized this by passing a statute authorizing the Supreme Court to issue the corresponding writ of "mandamus" against federal officers, including the Secretary of State.

However—and here was the catch—the Court found this authorization unconstitutional. Marbury had filed his complaint in the Supreme Court; in legal terms he was asking that court to exercise "original jurisdiction." In most cases, however, article III provides that the Supreme Court's jurisdiction is not "original" but "appellate"—the power to review decisions of other courts. The only exceptions listed in the Constitution are for cases in which, unlike *Marbury*, a state or a foreign diplomat is a party. The statute authorizing the Court to act as a trial court in mandamus cases, Marshall concluded, was therefore contrary to article III; and an unconstitutional statute could not be obeyed.

Thus the Supreme Court concluded that it had no power to right the government's wrong. Marbury never got his commission. Yet in denying their jurisdiction over this one small case the judges established the far more significant authority that has been the basis of constitutional decisionmaking down to the present day—their power to determine the constitutionality of acts of Congress.

Where did the judges get this authority? It was inherent, Marshall first argued, in the nature of a written constitution. "Certainly all those who have framed written constitutions," he wrote, "contemplate them as forming the fundamental and paramount law of the nation, and consequently, the theory of every such government must be, that an act of the legislature, repugnant to the constitution, is void." Moreover, the judges were required to resolve disputes, and to do so they had to decide what the law was. If a statute conflicted with the Constitution, the judge must apply one or the other; and since the Constitution was "superior to any ordinary act of the legislature, the constitution, and not such ordinary act, must govern the case to which they both apply." Finally, the explicit constitutional limitations on congressional authority would be worthless if the judges were required to obey unconstitutional laws: "It would be giving to the legislature a practical and real omnipotence, with the same breath which professes to restrict their powers within narrow limits. It is prescribing limits, and declaring that those limits may be passed at pleasure."

These arguments are clever but not decisive. The French Constitution of 1791 contradicted Marshall's generalization that judicial review was inseparable from a written constitution; a nineteenth-century observer noted critically that Marshall "assumes as an essential feature of a written constitution what does not exist [as of that time] in any one of the written constitutions of Europe."[2] In countries without judicial review, moreover, the judges must also resolve controversies; they do so by accepting the legislature's decision that its actions are constitutional. That this makes the legislature judge in its own case is not conclusive either. The fact that it is inadvisable to appoint foxes to guard chickens does not necessarily prove that the framers of the Constitution did not do so—especially since the question remains whether judicial review does not effectively place the judges themselves in the foxes' position.

Marshall invoked three specific provisions of the Constitution to support the structural arguments for judicial review already discussed. The first was article III, § 2, which extends the judicial power of the United States to "all cases . . . arising under this Constitution":

"Could it be the intention of those who gave this power, to say that in using it the constitution should not be looked into? That a case arising under the constitution should be decided without examining the instrument under which it arises? This is too extravagant to be maintained." Further, article VI requires the judges to swear "to support this Constitution"; "how immoral to impose [this oath] upon them," Marshall argued, "if they were to be used as the instruments . . . for violating what they swear to support!" Finally, as Marshall saw it, article VI declared not all federal statutes to be "the supreme law of the land," but only the constitutional ones—"those only which shall be made in *pursuance* of the constitution."

All three provisions, however, can be interpreted differently. The clause conferring jurisdiction over constitutional cases requires the judge to decide what the Constitution means; the oath requires him to do what the Constitution commands. Under a Constitution without judicial review, a refusal to invalidate federal statutes would satisfy both provisions.[3] The supremacy clause of article VI, in turn, speaks of laws enacted pursuant not to "*the* Constitution," as Marshall stated, but to "*this* Constitution." The additional words affording supremacy to "treaties *made, or which shall be made,*" strongly suggest that the purpose of the phrase "in pursuance" of "this Constitution" was not to distinguish constitutional from unconstitutional laws but rather to deny supremacy to laws made under our earlier Constitution, the Articles of Confederation.

Thus one cannot say that Marshall's arguments for judicial review of the constitutionality of federal statutes were wholly compelling. As a purely textual matter, however, Marshall's interpretation of the power to decide cases arising under the Constitution is at least as plausible as any other; and the record of the Constitutional Convention shows unmistakably that Marshall's conclusion is in accord with the intentions of the framers. In arguing against the creation of a Council of Revision to review federal statutes, for example, Rufus

King of Massachusetts insisted that "the Judges will have the ex-
pounding of those laws when they come before them; and they will
no doubt stop the operation of such as shall appear repugnant to the
Constitution."[4]

In any event, *Marbury v. Madison* is a basic source of the American doctrine of judicial review of both executive and legislative action, for in this case the judges confirmed their authority to determine both the legality of executive conduct and the constitutionality
of legislation.

SCOPE AND LIMITATIONS

The power of judicial review asserted in *Marbury v. Madison* is not
a monopoly of the Supreme Court. Because all federal and state
judges take an oath to support the Constitution, and because unconstitutional statutes are not the "law of the land," *every* judge must
refuse to enforce them. This obligation assures that the courts themselves cannot be used as instruments for infringing the constitutional
rights of the individual.

As Marshall recognized elsewhere in the *Marbury* opinion, however, the refusal of courts to cooperate in unconstitutional schemes is
not enough to protect the citizen from governmental oppression. It is
no comfort for a person who has been unlawfully arrested that the
courts did not authorize the government to seize him; he needs an affirmative court order requiring the government to set him free.

Accordingly, Congress has opened the federal courts to persons
complaining of unconstitutional government action. Pursuant to the
article III provision discussed in *Marbury*, Congress since 1875 has
authorized the federal trial courts to entertain cases "arising under the
Constitution." In such cases the courts have the power and duty to
afford redress against government officials who have invaded or
threatened to invade constitutional rights.[5]

There are nevertheless significant gaps in the authority of the judges to see to it that the Constitution is obeyed. In the first place, article III permits the federal courts to decide only "cases" and "controversies" of a traditional judicial character. This means, among other things, that there must be parties with a stake in the outcome on both sides of the case—in order, among other things, to assure that arguments on both sides are adequately presented. This requirement has been interpreted in such a way as to make certain kinds of statutes practically immune from judicial scrutiny.

The most familiar example is an appropriation law. Some years ago, for example, Congress passed a law authorizing the expenditure of federal funds to promote maternal health. Both the state of Massachusetts and a federal taxpayer brought suit, arguing that the Constitution gave Congress no power to spend money for such a purpose. The Supreme Court held it had no authority to decide the case, for neither the state nor the taxpayer was a proper party.

The state, which argued that Congress had usurped its authority, had only a "political" stake in the outcome, and that—partly for historical reasons—was held not to suffice. The taxpayer's interest was dismissed as "minute," "shared with millions of others," and unlikely to be affected by a decision that the expenditure was unconstitutional.[6]

Later decisions have allowed taxpayers to challenge expenditures that violate their *own* constitutional rights, such as the First Amendment right not to be taxed for religious purposes.[7] Most asserted limitations on the federal spending power, however, serve to protect the interests not of the taxpayer but of the states, and in general a complainant may not assert the rights of others. The upshot is that most federal spending measures cannot be challenged in court at all, for no one has the requisite "standing to sue."

Judicial review is further limited by the principle of "sovereign immunity," which precludes suits against either the states or the United States without their consent. This unfortunate principle finds its expression in part in the Eleventh Amendment, which—in response to a contrary Supreme Court decision[8]—forbids suit against one state by a citizen of another.

As the Supreme Court later recognized, this amendment merely confirmed the broader intentions of the framers of the original Constitution. As noted above, the "cases" and "controversies" over which federal courts have jurisdiction are those which were traditionally decided by courts; and neither in England nor in the states had the government been suable without its consent. As James Madison told the Virginia ratifying convention in explaining article III's provision for federal jurisdiction over controversies between states and citizens of other states, "[i]t is not in the power of individuals to call any state into court. The only operation [this provision] can have, is that, if a state should wish to bring a suit against a citizen, it must be brought before the federal court."[9]

The United States has waived its immunity from suit in many classes of cases,[10] but Congress could withdraw its consent to be sued at any time. Only occasionally have states voluntarily surrendered their immunity from federal suits,[11] and even Congress may lift *state* immunity only in cases arising under certain constitutional amendments—on the theory that these amendments implicitly modified the preexisting immunity principle.[12]

Suits against government *officers* often have the same impact on the government as if it had been sued by name. Nevertheless, in order to reduce the devastating effect of sovereign immunity on judicial protection of constitutional rights, the Court has held that a suit to forbid an officer to violate such rights in the future is not a suit against the state for purposes of immunity.[13]

This fiction was too much to swallow, however, in cases in which the complaint sought to compel the officer to remedy a wrong for which only the state was legally responsible, or to take action only the state could take. Consequently it remains true today that a litigant cannot avoid the state's immunity in a suit to recover damages for past wrongs from the state treasury by labeling it as a suit against an individual officer.[14]

Third, despite *Marbury v. Madison* the Supreme Court has often alluded to the existence of a shadowy category of "political questions" that the judges will refuse to decide even if they arise in a concrete controversy between an interested plaintiff and a suable defendant. It was on this ground that the Court refused to decide, for example, whether the adoption of laws by popular initiative was consistent with article IV's guarantee of "a republican form of government," or how much time the states had to ratify a constitutional amendment proposed by Congress.[15]

The mere fact that an issue has political significance, of course, is not enough to make it a nonjusticiable "political question." A great many of the constitutional questions the courts have unhesitatingly decided, including the question of judicial review itself, are of enormous political importance.

The political-question concept had its origin in *Marbury v. Madison*, where Chief Justice Marshall emphatically denied any judicial competence to resolve "questions in their nature political." The context strongly suggests that with this phrase Marshall meant only to emphasize his conclusion that the judges must not intrude upon the area of discretion reserved to another branch of government. This conclusion makes eminent sense; by definition an officer who acts within his legal authority infringes no legal right.

Some "political question" decisions can be explained on this ground. Article V, it may be argued, leaves it entirely to Congress to determine the time during which a proposed amendment may be approved; it imposes no time limit of its own. In cases like this the political-question label disguises what is in fact a decision on the merits of the claim, not a refusal to decide.[16]

In other cases an issue may be classified as "political" because the

Constitution deliberately excluded the ordinary courts from resolving it. One frequently cited example is the question whether a federal officer has committed "high crimes and misdemeanors" justifying his removal from office, for under article I, § 3 only the Senate is empowered to make this decision.[17] It was on similar grounds that the Court justified its refusal to decide whether lawmaking by popular initiative offended the Guarantee Clause of article IV.

Some Justices have argued that the "political question" concept is not limited to the above types of cases but includes other issues that for one reason or another are unusually sensitive or for whose resolution "judicially manageable standards" are lacking.[18] Justice Felix Frankfurter, for example, argued that the courts should not pass upon the apportionment of legislative seats within a single state even on the assumption that some parts of the state were so underrepresented as to deny their inhabitants the equal protection of the laws.[19]

The majority disagreed, partly because it thought the command of the Equal Protection Clause was clear; and the court-ordered reapportionments of the past thirty-five years have been one of the great success stories of our constitutional history.[20] It seems unlikely that Chief Justice Marshall would have agreed with Frankfurter's sweeping version of the political-question doctrine, for it detracts substantially from what Marshall described as the fundamental principle that for every right there must be a judicial remedy. It is encouraging that in recent years the Court has shown little inclination to employ the political-question notion in Frankfurter's broad sense.[21]

Finally, it is not clear to what extent other branches of the federal government may limit the power of judicial review. It is true that article III extends the judicial power to all cases arising under the Constitution, and that neither Congress nor the President may alter the Constitution itself. Yet the Constitution expressly empowers Congress to make "exceptions" to the Supreme Court's appellate jurisdiction and seems not to require that there be lower federal courts at all;

for it vests judicial power only in the Supreme Court and "such inferior courts as the Congress from time to time may ordain and establish." On the basis of these provisions there have been suggestions in Supreme Court opinions that Congress may limit the jurisdiction of federal courts—and thereby effectively preclude judicial review—at pleasure.[22]

These broad observations, however, do not qualify as binding precedent, for they went further than was necessary to justify the Court's decisions. It is clear, in fact, that Congress may not so limit the jurisdiction of the courts as to require judges to enforce statutes without passing upon their constitutionality. Even on its narrowest possible interpretation, *Marbury v. Madison* forbids the judges themselves to enforce unconstitutional laws.[23]

Moreover, *Marbury* also stated a broader and even more important principle: Judicial review is an indispensable element of the constitutional system of checks and balances designed to prevent other branches of government from usurping authority. The power of Congress to limit the jurisdiction of the courts should not be so broadly construed as to permit the lawmakers to destroy this intended check on their own limited powers.[24]

The same holds true for other methods of undermining judicial review. In 1805 President Jefferson attempted to remove political enemies from the bench by impeachment; 130 years later President Franklin Roosevelt sought to drown out discordant judicial voices by the appointment of additional Justices.[25] Jefferson ran aground on the text of article II, § 4, which requires no mere difference of opinion but "high crimes and misdemeanors" before judges can be removed. Roosevelt's "court packing" plan encountered stiff resistance in the Senate, but he abandoned it only after the Justices reversed themselves and stopped obstructing his "New Deal" measures for relieving the Great Depression.[26] In each of these cases, one can argue, the President's plan was contrary to the spirit of *Marbury v. Madison.*

We return finally to the fundamental question left unanswered earlier in this chapter: Would a more complete system of judicial review leave us with too little protection against the *judges?* The provisions of article V afford some measure of consolation: The intended remedy for judicial usurpation is amendment of the Constitution itself.

3   *Federalism*

A s noted in chapter i, the Constitution gives the central govern ment a limited list of powers. To avoid any misunder-
standing, the Tenth Amendment expressly provides that all powers
not granted to the United States are reserved to the states.

Outside the field of military and foreign affairs, federal authority
does not appear to be very extensive. Supporters of the Constitution,
moreover, uniformly assured the country that this appearance was not
deceiving. "The powers delegated to the Federal Government," James
Madison insisted, "are few and defined," those "to remain in the State
Governments . . . numerous and indefinite."[1]

The limited nature of federal authority reflected not only the conviction that local government was more likely to deal knowledgeably
with local problems but also the fear that a strong central government
would be dangerous to liberty. If the government of a single state falls
into bad hands, one can move elsewhere; if the government of the
whole nation is oppressive, there is no place to run.

Interpretation, however, has given a surprisingly broad scope to
the catalog of congressional powers. This development is the principal subject of the present chapter.

Federal Powers

The story begins with the famous case of *McCulloch v. Maryland*
in 1819.[2] Congress had established a national bank, and Maryland attempted to tax it. The bank refused to pay the tax, and a bank em-
ployee was punished for the refusal. The Supreme Court set the
penalty aside: Congress had power to establish the bank, and the tax
was unconstitutional.

Chief Justice Marshall conceded that Congress had only the powers the Constitution gave it, and the Constitution nowhere mentioned banks. Article I, however, expressly confirmed that the various
powers granted to Congress carried with them authority to enact all
laws "necessary and proper" to their execution. A law might be "necessary and proper," Marshall concluded, without being indispensable.
"Let the end be legitimate"—let its goal be the exercise of some power
entrusted to the Federal Government—"and all means which are appropriate, which are plainly adapted to that end, which are not prohibited, but consist with the letter and spirit of the constitution, are
constitutional."

This carefully composed interpretation still defines the extent of
congressional power. However, it is extremely general; everything depends upon how it is applied. In 1870, for example, a divided
Supreme Court professing to follow Marshall's test held that a requirement that creditors accept paper money in payment of debts was
not "necessary and proper" either to federal borrowing or to the conduct of the Civil War. The next year, after two new Justices had been
appointed, a majority applied the same test to reach the opposite result, concluding—as Marshall himself had insisted—that Congress
had a choice among means of achieving its legitimate goals.[3]

Marshall spent little time in *McCulloch* explaining to which of
Congress's powers the establishment of the bank was "necessary and
proper," or why it was an "appropriate" means to those ends. Elsewhere in the opinion he had mentioned in passing the authority to
collect taxes, borrow money, support armies, and regulate commerce
among the states. Others had argued convincingly that the bank
would promote both borrowing and tax collection and that bank-
notes would facilitate interstate commerce.[4]

The ostensibly narrow grant of authority to Congress to regulate
"commerce with foreign nations, and among the several states, and
with the Indian tribes," to which Marshall referred in *McCulloch*, had

not been controversial. Dissatisfaction with state obstruction of interstate and foreign trade had been one of the principal reasons for calling the Constitutional Convention; everyone seemed to agree that Congress should be authorized to protect commerce from parochial state restrictions. In rebutting antifederalist arguments that the Constitution would unduly centralize power, James Madison had felt no need to defend the Commerce Clause, noting that it seemed to be one provision "from which no apprehensions are entertained."[5] It proved in fact to be a time bomb.

The Supreme Court's interpretation of this clause began innocuously enough in 1824 with the unsurprising conclusion in *Gibbons v. Ogden* that commerce included not only the buying and selling of goods but the interstate transportation of passengers as well.[6] In this case, as in *McCulloch*, Marshall emphasized the limited nature of congressional power. Not even all *commerce*, he correctly observed, was subject to federal regulation; "[t]he completely internal commerce of a state . . . may be considered as reserved for the state itself."

As early as 1838, however, the Court went a giant step further in upholding a federal law punishing the theft of shipwrecked goods. It was not necessary, wrote Justice Joseph Story, that the thief himself be engaged in interstate or foreign commerce; the law was "necessary and proper" to protect that commerce from outside interference.[7]

Later decisions continued this development. Railroad cars without safety devices endangered interstate traffic even if they traveled only within a single state.[8] Low rates for local transportation diverted goods that might otherwise have been shipped from one state to another.[9] Even wheat planted to feed a farmer's own livestock depressed the demand and thus the price in interstate trade. If the farmer did not grow his own wheat, the Court argued, he would have to buy it; and he might buy wheat that was grown in another state.[10] Thus all these local matters *affected* interstate or foreign commerce. Anything with such an effect, the Court concluded, was subject to congressional regulation; and virtually everything has such an effect in a modern society.

The interpretation of other congressional powers underwent a similar development. Because soldiers need grain and intoxicated workers produce inferior weapons, the Court held a ban on the production of alcoholic beverages necessary and proper to the raising and supporting of armies.[11] Because the Justices were unwilling to look behind a purported exercise of the tax power to find an illegitimate purpose, they permitted Congress to protect dairymen from competition by imposing a prohibitive tax on margarine.[12] Because article I authorizes Congress to lay taxes in order to promote the general welfare, the Court allowed Congress to require a state to raise the drinking age to 21 as a condition of obtaining federal highway funds.[13] Given the practical importance of federal grants today, the power to impose conditions enables Congress effectively to regulate anything it pleases.

The path to this state of affairs was not a straight one. From time to time, over many years, the judges would unpredictably declare federal statutes unconstitutional on the ground that otherwise there would be no effective limit to congressional power.[14] A series of decisions striking down New Deal economic measures, however, led to President Roosevelt's 1937 proposal to pack the Court with additional Justices of his own persuasion, and the Court capitulated entirely.

Federalism still lives in Congress. Out of respect for state interests, there are still relatively few federal laws in the important fields of private law (including commercial and accident law, corporations, and domestic relations) and even crime. For a number of years, however, in light of the developments described above, it appeared that this congressional restraint was no longer attributable to constitutional compulsion. In spite of the unambiguous terms of the Constitution and the equally unambiguous intentions of its authors, the powers of Congress seemed no longer to be significantly limited by federalistic concerns.

The apparent collapse of constitutional federalism was attributable not only to the perceived needs of a modern society but also to
the tension between two constitutional principles that Chief Justice
Marshall had identified in *McCulloch v. Maryland.* On the one hand,
the central government was authorized to take all measures necessary
to effectuate its granted powers; on the other, much domestic civil authority was meant to be reserved to the states.

Some of the Supreme Court's more extreme interpretations of federal power could easily have been avoided. The Court could readily
have concluded, for example, that the protection of butter producers
from competition was not a legitimate federal goal in the sense of the
McCulloch standard. "[S]hould Congress, under the *pretext* of executing its powers, pass laws for the accomplishment of objects not entrusted to the government," Marshall had said in that case, "it would
be the painful duty of this tribunal . . . to say that such an act was not
the law of the land."

Similarly, in light of its history the clause empowering Congress to
"lay and collect taxes . . . to pay the debts and provide for the common defense and general welfare of the United States" need not have
been construed to authorize expenditures for purposes beyond those
otherwise entrusted to the federal government. The Articles of Confederation had provided that "all charges of war and all other expenses, that shall be incurred for the common defense or general welfare, . . . shall be defrayed out of a common treasury, which shall be
supplied by the several states . . . ." This provision clearly provided
only for the method of paying obligations authorized by other provisions of the articles; juxtaposition of the articles with the Constitution suggests that the only change intended was that expenses be paid
out of taxes rather than out of contributions from the states.[15]

The proper scope of the Commerce Clause, however, cannot so
neatly be determined. The decisions cited above suggest that there are
no firm logical distinctions between the cases lying on opposite sides

of the intended boundary. *McCulloch's* federalistic "spirit of the Constitution" tells us only that a line must be drawn somewhere; it does not tell us where a defensible line can be drawn.

Nevertheless it was in the slippery field of interstate commerce, not taxing and spending, that the Supreme Court in the 1995 case of *United States v. Lopez* finally called a halt to the expansion of federal authority.[16] Earlier decisions upholding Congress's power to regulate local transactions, Chief Justice William Rehnquist explained, had dealt with "economic activity"; they did not support a statute making it a federal crime to carry guns in school.

Just where the Court's newfound respect for state rights will lead remains to be seen; two Justices whose votes were necessary to the result wrote separately to emphasize that no departure from earlier decisions was intended. It is refreshing all the same to discover that there are still cases in which the judges will enforce the Constitution's plain principle that not all powers are given to the federal government.

THE COMMERCE CLAUSE AND STATE AUTHORITY

Article I, § 8 gives Congress "exclusive" authority to legislate for the District of Columbia. Article I, § 10 expressly excludes the states from certain other areas of congressional competence; no state may coin money, for example, or make treaties. In contrast to these provisions stands the Commerce Clause, which grants Congress authority to regulate interstate and foreign commerce *without* explicitly excluding the possibility of concurrent state regulation.

On the basis of similar language, the Supreme Court came very early to the conclusion that the clause empowering Congress to enact "uniform laws on the subject of bankruptcies" did not forbid the states to enact insolvency laws of their own.[17] The Commerce Clause could well have been read the same way: When the framers of the Constitution meant to make federal authority exclusive, they said so.[18]

Before the Constitution was adopted, however, the states had se-

riously impeded interstate commerce by subjecting it to burdensome
taxes and restrictions, and the purpose of the clause was to remove ob-
stacles to interstate trade erected by state law.[19] In light of this purpose the Supreme Court long ago concluded that the Commerce
Clause *did* limit state power to burden interstate or foreign commerce
through regulation or taxation.[20] This was not a necessary conclusion.
The text of the clause, coupled with an explicit restriction of state im-
port or export taxes (art. I, § 10), suggests that in most cases freedom
of trade was to be achieved through protective federal legislation
rather than through constitutional limitations.

Because the states often had legitimate interests in regulating or
taxing interstate or international activities, the Court did not exclude
the states from this field altogether. As a result there have been great
numbers of decisions determining whether particular measures unac-
ceptably burdened interstate or foreign commerce, and the judges
have enunciated a variety of criteria for making this determination.

In earlier days the Court said variously that the states could never
regulate commerce but could *affect* it by noncommercial measures enacted under their undefined "police power"; that they could regulate
commerce itself when there was no need for uniform federal regulation; and that they could regulate commerce only "indirectly."[21] More
recently the Court has tended to acknowledge that the question can
be resolved only by a balancing of opposing interests: How serious is
the burden on commerce, and how weighty is the state's concern?[22]

This formulation leaves a great deal to the judgment of the courts.
Several rules of thumb, however, have effectively narrowed the judges'
freedom of decision. In the first place, it is seldom possible to justify
a state law that actually *discriminates* against interstate commerce in
favor of local interests, such as a tax *solely* on out-of-state products. In
the intended common market, goods from other states must be allowed to compete on equal terms.[23] For the same reason the Court
looks with particular suspicion on any sort of taxes that two or more

states might impose on a single interstate transaction, such as a flat fee for transporting goods; for multiple taxation too places interstate commerce at a competitive disadvantage.[24]

In general, moreover, state interests in protecting health and safety are given more weight than the interest in regulating the market for purely economic reasons. A state may limit the number of trucks using its highways in order to promote traffic safety, for example, but not in order to restrict competition.[25]

Even safety concerns, however, do not always justify a serious impediment to commerce. Because wide trucks posed a genuine danger on narrow highways, the states were allowed to forbid them; but they were not allowed to outlaw long trains, because the resulting safety advantages were doubtful and the burden on commerce great.[26]

INTERGOVERNMENTAL IMMUNITIES

McCulloch v. Maryland established a second implicit limitation on state authority: the states had no power to tax the Bank of the United States.

The Court made little effort to show where this limitation was found in the Constitution. Chief Justice Marshall did mention the Supremacy Clause of article VI, which makes federal law supreme in case of conflict; but he identified no provision of federal law with which the state tax conflicted.

Marshall made quite clear the *practical* ground for his conclusion: "The power to tax involves the power to destroy." If the states could tax the National Bank, they could destroy it; and the framers never intended the federal government to be at the mercy of the states. The same reasoning later led the Court to hold the states without power to *regulate* the federal government.[27]

Marshall was not deterred from his conclusion by the fact that the Bank of the United States was a largely private institution; it sufficed that the bank served to carry out functions of the central government.

Nor did he rely on the fact that the tax in question placed the bank at a disadvantage by exempting its local competitors, arguing instead that any inquiry into the nature of the particular exaction was "unfit for the judicial department." Justice Holmes's riposte in arguing against an extension of the immunity recognized in *McCulloch* was telling: "The power to tax is not the power to destroy while this Court sits."[28]

There is a more fundamental argument, however, against the entire principle of federal immunity from state laws. Marshall was right that the framers could hardly have meant to allow the states to destroy the federal government, but no constitutional immunity was necessary to prevent that from happening. Even if the Constitution itself provided no immunity, Congress could protect the bank from destructive state taxation by legislation under the Necessary and Proper Clause.[29]

Did *McCulloch* require the converse conclusion that the United States could not tax the states? The states were equally essential components of the Union, and federal taxes could destroy them too. Marshall nevertheless hesitated to approve a corresponding limitation of the taxing power of Congress. When a state taxed the nation, he argued, it largely taxed the citizens of other states, who had no say in the taxing decision. The states, in contrast, had Representatives and Senators in Congress to protect their interests against the central government; they needed no constitutional protection.

The Tenth Amendment and the careful enumeration of limited federal powers, however, demonstrate that the framers of the Constitution were not content to rely on political checks but considered constitutional limitations necessary to protect the states from federal aggrandizement. Moreover, the states actually need a constitutional immunity from taxation or regulation far more than the nation does. Because federal law is paramount, the states cannot, like the United States, protect themselves by statute. Consequently the Supreme Court later concluded, despite Marshall, that Congress could not tax the states either.[30]

In recent years the Supreme Court has significantly relaxed the limitations on intergovernmental taxation and regulation. The United States may now tax the salaries of state employees, and vice-versa, although such taxes indirectly increase the cost of governing.[31] Congress may tax the state itself like any other person, if for example it sells mineral water,[32] and federal minimum-wage laws may now apply to state employees.[33] One Justice has even argued that the immunity recognized in *McCulloch* itself was based not upon the Constitution but upon the bank's statutory charter.[34]

Intergovernmental immunity has not disappeared entirely, however. Whether the basis is statutory or constitutional, it remains the law that the states have no power to impede the exercise of federal authority either by taxation or otherwise, although the Constitution does not say so explicitly. The related immunity of states from suit, as noted in the preceding chapter, is alive and well. Finally, in recent years the Court has made clear that, although Congress may regulate the activities of the states themselves, it may not coopt state legislatures or executive officers to enforce federal law against private parties; for the states are not administrative departments of the federal government.[35]

4   *The Separation of Powers*

T HE FIRST THREE ARTICLES of the Constitution vest the federal legislative power in Congress, the executive power in the President, and the judicial power in the courts. The boundaries between legislative, executive, and judicial powers, however, are not always easy to discern.

THE RULE OF LAW

The border between congressional and presidential powers occupied the Supreme Court in the famous 1952 case of *Youngstown Sheet & Tube Co. v. Sawyer*.[1] During the Korean War, the steelworkers threatened to strike for better terms of employment. In order to avoid interruption of the flow of military supplies, President Truman took temporary possession of the steel mills, for it was illegal to strike against the government. On a complaint filed by the mill owners, the Supreme Court held that the President had acted unconstitutionally.

Four of the nine Justices were of the opinion that Congress had implicitly forbidden seizure of the steel mills by prescribing a distinct remedy for strikes that endangered national security.[2] For these judges it was sufficient to invoke the fundamental principle of the supremacy of law. Article I's grant of lawmaking authority to Congress implies that the executive and judicial branches are bound by the statutes that Congress enacts. This implication is underscored by articles VI and II, which respectively designate such statutes as "supreme law of the land" and direct the President to "take care" that they "be faithfully executed."

It is true that Congress has no power to deprive the President of the authority the Constitution gives him. Only the President, for example, may be commander in chief of the armed forces.[3] How the President executes the laws, on the other hand, may to some extent be determined by legislation pursuant to the Necessary and Proper Clause.[4] Thus in the narrowest sense the *Youngstown* decision merely confirms that the President must obey the law and that Congress may limit presidential authority to seize private property even for purposes of national security.

The reasoning of the Court's opinion, however, went further. The President, wrote Justice Hugo Black, had only those powers conferred by the Constitution. As commander in chief, he had extensive authority on the battlefield. In ordinary domestic matters, however, he was empowered only to execute the laws, and no law authorized him to seize the steel mills. Only Congress, Justice Robert Jackson added, was authorized to "raise and support armies" and thus to provide for supplying them.

With these words the Supreme Court announced an important aspect of the Rule of Law that went beyond the simple duty of other branches to obey laws actually passed by Congress. *Only* Congress may adopt federal laws; and in most cases even the President may act only on the basis of law.

This principle is implicit not only in the enumeration of limited presidential powers in article II, but in article I's list of congressional powers as well. Congress was given authority to raise and support armies, for example, because the framers of the Constitution trusted no one but the elected representatives of the people to make such a fundamental decision, and because separating support and command authority protected against arbitrary action by any single branch.[5]

Additional support for the principle that the President may act only on the basis of law is found, as Justice Robert Jackson argued, in the Fifth Amendment's provision forbidding the government to deprive any person of life, liberty, or property without "due process of law," which was based upon a section of Magna Carta permitting invasions of individual rights only in accordance with "the law of the land." In directing the President to "take care that the laws be faithfully executed," Jackson wrote, article II "gives a governmental authority that reaches so far as there is law"; in forbidding deprivations of life, liberty, or property without due process the Fifth Amendment "gives a private right that authority shall go no further."[6]

In a dissenting opinion, three Justices protested that the powers of the President were not confined to commanding the armed forces and executing the laws. The first section of article II, they insisted, conferred on the President the entire "executive power" of the United States. This power, in their view, was not limited to the enumerated subjects that followed, but embraced everything that executive officers traditionally had done. On the basis of this authority, they concluded, Presidents from the beginning had done whatever was necessary to protect the general welfare in an emergency.

As argued above, however, the structure and history of the Constitution strongly suggest that in domestic matters article II gave the President no general executive authority, but only the executive powers specifically enumerated. This is clearly the case with respect to Congress, which is given only the "legislative powers herein granted."[7] Article II contains no such unambiguous limitation, but a general executive power would fit very poorly into the overall constitutional plan.

No one denied that long-accepted practice could help to establish the constitutionality of actions whose legality had as an original matter been doubtful. Justice Frankfurter, for example, conceded that such a practice could amount to a "gloss" on the Constitution, and the Supreme Court had often relied on the practice of other branches in addition to its own precedents to support the constitutionality of challenged action.[8] The dissenters in *Youngstown*, however, were unable to show such a practice with respect to emergency executive authority; most of their purported examples missed the mark.

The familiar Emancipation Proclamation, by which President Lincoln freed slaves living behind Confederate lines during the Civil War, was a battlefield measure of the commander in chief. In virtually all other cases involving private rights the President had acted on the basis of statutory authority, as in exercising his express statutory right to suppress insurrections by military force. The most doubtful incident cited by the dissenters before the eve of the Second World War was President Roosevelt's dramatic closing of the nation's banks during the Great Depression to prevent their financial collapse—and even that was based on purported statutory authority. A single example in a century and a half hardly constitutes longstanding acquiescence in the existence of general emergency powers.

The dissenters further argued that in seizing the mills President Truman had acted within his authority to execute the laws, since statutes provided both for supplying the armed forces and for combating inflation. None of these laws, however, authorized the President to seize private property in order to achieve their purposes. The issue thus was whether article II empowered the President to employ all suitable means of enforcing the laws that Congress had not actually prohibited, or only those means which Congress itself had approved.

Two important nineteenth-century decisions speak for a broad interpretation of the power to execute laws. The first was *In re Neagle*,[9] where the Supreme Court confirmed the President's power without specific statutory authority to appoint marshals to protect federal judges who applied the laws. The second was *In re Debs*,[10] upholding the President's nonstatutory power to seek an injunction against a strike that threatened interstate commerce. Justice Black seems to have thought either that these decisions were no longer law or that they were not analogous to the *Youngstown* case.

Since four of the Justices in the majority believed that Congress had prohibited the seizure, the question of the scope of the power to employ means of execution neither authorized nor forbidden was not definitively answered. *Youngstown* is nevertheless a landmark case affirming not only that the President must obey the law but that in general he may act only on the basis of statutory authority.

MILITARY POWERS

Under the *Youngstown* decision, Congress raises and supplies the armed forces, while the President commands them. Does this mean that it is the President who decides whether or not to engage in hostilities?

Article I, § 8 gives *Congress* the power "to declare war." The evident reason for this provision is to assure that, like the decision to raise an army, the even more critical decision to go to war is made by the representatives of the people.[11] Presidential authority to introduce troops into hostilities at will would undermine this purpose.

Is the President then powerless to respond to an attack on the United States until Congress declares war? The Convention record confirms the suspicion that the Constitution is not so suicidal. The original proposal was to authorize Congress "to *make* war"; the present language was substituted for the express purpose of assuring that the commander in chief could "repel sudden attacks."[12] In this spirit Congress, acting pursuant to explicit authority conferred by article I, § 8, has authorized the President to employ armed force to defend the United States against insurrection or invasion.[13]

In spite of the constitutional text and its history, a number of Presidents in this century have introduced troops into hostile situations on numerous occasions on which there appeared to be no immediate military threat to the United States. Even before the First World War, President Wilson sent troops to Vera Cruz during the Mexican Revolution. In the 1950s and 60s various Presidents dispatched massive forces to defend South Korea and South Vietnam. President Carter sent helicopters to rescue hostages in Iran; President Reagan invaded the island nation of Grenada to put down an extremist coup and bombed Tripoli in 1986 in response to alleged Libyan terrorism; President Clinton bombed Iraq and Serbia—the latter in response to "ethnic cleansing" in Kosovo.[14]

Did all these Presidents exceed their authority, or have we here a practice legitimized by long acquiescence, as the dissenting Justices argued in *Youngstown*? All attempts to obtain a Supreme Court ruling as to the legality of the war in Vietnam were fruitless. Without invoking the "political question" doctrine discussed in chapter 2, the Court exercised its discretion to decline jurisdiction over cases raising this issue—doubtless in the conviction that the problem was too politically explosive to be settled by judicial decision.[15]

In 1973 Congress, which had indirectly supported the Korean and Vietnamese adventures by providing military appropriations, adopted the so-called War Powers Resolution in an effort to defend its own military prerogatives.[16] This resolution does not purport to limit the President's constitutional powers; Congress has no authority to do that. It does attempt to *define* the relative spheres of presidential and congressional authority in a way that corresponds to the original understanding rather than to recent practice.

The President may introduce troops into hostilities, according to Congress's interpretation, only pursuant to statutory authorization or to a declaration of war, or in the event of an attack on the United States or its armed forces. This construction binds neither the President nor the judges, who under *Marbury v. Madison* must interpret the Constitution for themselves.[17] The views of Congress, however, are surely of importance when other branches undertake the task of interpretation.

Before the President takes military action, the resolution requires him "in every possible instance" to "consult with Congress." This provision raises interesting questions. In the Libyan controversy, for example, the President disclosed his plans only after the bombers were in the air, and only to a few leading members of Congress. A few members are arguably not "Congress"; they had precious little time to reflect on the merits of the project; and it is not clear what would have happened if they had objected to the bombing. If consultation is deemed not "possible" because of the ever-present need for secrecy, moreover, the entire provision is without practical significance.

Whether or not prior consultation is possible, the resolution also requires the President to inform Congress within forty-eight hours after introducing troops on his own initiative. At the end of sixty days he must withdraw the troops unless Congress has declared war or extended the deadline, or is unable to meet. Even during this sixty-day period, moreover, he is required to withdraw them if Congress directs him to do so.

Are these provisions constitutional? Congress relied upon article I, § 8, which authorizes it to enact all laws necessary and proper to the exercise of the President's as well as its own powers. President Nixon, whose veto of the resolution was overridden by Congress, argued that it unconstitutionally restricted his defensive authority. The evident purpose of this authority, however, was to allow the President to defend the country in an emergency. That the President's power was based upon the need to respond to *sudden* attacks emphasizes the intention of the framers that ultimate authority to decide between peace and war rests with Congress; the President should act only to preserve the status quo until Congress is in a position to decide.

The War Powers Resolution is fully in accord with this interpretation. President Truman's famous words after the steel-seizure decision nevertheless carry great practical weight: "Whatever the six Justices of the Supreme Court meant by their differing opinions, [the President] must always act in a national emergency."

INDEPENDENT AGENCIES

Article I entrusts the legislative power to Congress, so that national policy will be determined by the democratically elected representatives of the people. Article II vests the executive power in the President in the interest of a unified and electorally responsible administration. Article III grants the judicial power to independent judges with virtual life tenure, so that disputes may be decided on their merits without fear of reprisal. Above all, the dispersion of federal authority among three separate branches serves as a significant protection against arbitrary action by any organ of government.[18]

Yet there are federal agencies today that appear to exercise all three of these functions, although their officers are neither democratically elected, nor subject to presidential control, nor protected by indefinite tenure.

In 1914, for example, in order to carry out a statutory ban on "unfair methods of competition," Congress created the Federal Trade Commission, a body largely independent of all three branches. Members of the Commission are appointed for seven-year terms and removable by the President only for "inefficiency, neglect of duty, or malfeasance in office." The Commission defines the forbidden competitive methods by promulgating general rules, issues complaints against offenders, and decides after formal hearing whether it has proved its own case.[19] In so doing the Commission appears to exercise legislative, executive, and judicial powers all at once, contrary to Articles I, II, and III, and to the basic principle of separation of powers.[20]

Under existing Supreme Court precedents, however, the Commission is pretty clearly constitutional.

First, the Court has expressly declared that the Commission's authority to define unfair trade practices does not give it legislative power in violation of article I.[21] It is true that the Court has always insisted that Congress may not delegate the lawmaking responsibility entrusted to it by the Constitution, but must make the basic policy decisions itself. Half a century ago, indeed, the Justices declared two statutory provisions unconstitutional because they delegated largely unrestrained policymaking authority to the President.[22] This does not mean, however, that Congress may never authorize other organs of government to promulgate general rules or regulations. All enforcement agencies must interpret and define the inevitably general terms of the laws they enforce. To this extent the articulation of governing norms is an integral part of the executive rather than the legislative power. According to the decisions, it is enough that Congress has laid down a "primary standard" or an "intelligible principle" to which the enforcing agency is required to conform.[23]

For decades, moreover, the Supreme Court has given Congress considerable latitude in this regard, upholding, among other things, a statute empowering the executive to recover "excessive profits," which the statute did not define, from government suppliers.[24] The Commission's statutory mandate to define "unfair methods of competition" states a no less "intelligible principle."

Second, the Supreme Court has squarely held that despite their ostensibly executive powers the Commissioners need not be subject to presidential control. In *Myers v. United States*, in 1926, the Court had emphasized article II's principle of unified administration in striking down a statute requiring the consent of the Senate before the President could remove a postmaster.[25] Nine years later, however, in *Humphrey's Executor v. United States*, the Court unanimously upheld the provision forbidding the President to discharge Federal Trade Commissioners except for "inefficiency, neglect of duty, or malfeasance in office."[26] Principally, the Court reasoned, the Commission acted in a "quasi-judicial" or "quasi-legislative" capacity; any authority it had to execute the laws was only "incidental" to the fulfillment of its nonexecutive functions.

This argument is not convincing. Even if the Court were right about "quasi-judicial" and "quasi-legislative" powers, that would not justify giving independent Commissioners the plainly executive authority to file and prosecute complaints. As the Court observed in the postmaster's case, the President cannot fulfill his constitutional obligation to "take care that the laws be faithfully executed" if he cannot control those who actually enforce them.

Moreover, if Congress may grant quasi-legislative and quasi-judicial functions to a commission, it is only because they are *neither* legislative nor judicial, for the former belong to Congress and the latter to the courts. That means that they too are executive and may be exercised only by officers subject to presidential control—for the Constitution recognizes only legislative, judicial, and executive powers.

When the Court upheld Congress's authority to provide for appointment of special prosecutors independent of presidential control in *Morrison v. Olson* in 1988, it abandoned its specious reliance on quasi-judicial and quasi-legislative functions; it sufficed that the prosecutors' functions were not "central" to the President's duties.[27] Justice Scalia's lone dissent was unanswerable: The Constitution vests the executive power in the President, and prosecution is an executive power.

Finally, despite article III the Supreme Court has concluded that administrative agencies may decide cases or controversies that fall within the judicial power, provided that (as in the case of the Federal Trade Commission) the administrative decision is subject to judicial review.[28]

The statutory authority of the courts to correct errors in quasi-judicial administrative decisions, however, is extremely limited. In most instances the courts may set aside neither the agency's findings of fact nor its application of the law to the facts simply because they are wrong, but only if they are wholly unreasonable.[29] The practical result is thus that there are federal trial judges who are not protected by life tenure or irreducible salary, despite the unmistakable terms and purpose of article III.[30]

Apart from the unfortunate special-prosecutor decision and the holding in *Clinton v. Jones* permitting the President to be distracted by private lawsuits during his term of office,[31] the Justices in recent years have taken significant steps toward restoring the intended separation of powers. They have construed a rulemaking authorization narrowly to avoid finding that it delegated arguably legislative authority.[32] They have held that Congress may set aside administrative action only by the constitutionally prescribed process of legislation and not by a single house's "legislative veto."[33] They have held that Congress may neither appoint nor remove officers with authority to execute the laws.[34] They have concluded that bankruptcy judges must enjoy the independence guaranteed by article III in order to decide certain kinds of controversies even at the trial level.[35] Finally, as noted in chapter 1, they have decisively blocked an attempted end run around the Constitution's unmistakable refusal to give the President an item veto; as George Washington recognized in the 1790s, he must approve a bill in toto or not at all.[36]

Like federalism after the *Lopez* decision, the separation of federal powers is still a viable constitutional principle. The decisions demonstrate, however, that federal powers are by no means so strictly separated as the text and history of the Constitution would lead us to believe.

5   *Due Process of Law*

THE PRECEDING CHAPTERS dealt principally with the division of authority between the United States and the states and among the various branches of the federal government. We turn now to investigation of those constitutional provisions that protect the citizen directly from government abuse. We begin with the mysterious clauses of the Fifth and Fourteenth Amendments that forbid the United States and the states respectively to "deprive any person of life, liberty, or property without due process of law."

PROCEDURAL REQUIREMENTS

"Due process of law," the Supreme Court said in its first encounter with the Fifth Amendment provision in 1856, meant the traditional procedures of the common law.[1] From the beginning, as the text seems to suggest, the Due Process Clauses have been employed to assure that no one is deprived of life, liberty, or property except by a suitable *process*—that is, by an appropriate procedure.

The strict historical test the Court first enunciated, however, did not long survive. Sensibly doubting that the framers of the amendments meant to freeze the details of preexisting procedure for all time, the Court held first that not all common-law procedural rights were "fundamental" enough to qualify as requisites of due process and then that the common law was insufficient in some respects to satisfy current due process standards.[2] More recent decisions have tended to equate due process with a procedure that is fundamentally fair.[3]

In a criminal proceeding, for example, the defendant is entitled to notice and an opportunity to be heard before an unbiased and unintimidated judge. The prosecution must prove guilt beyond a reasonable doubt without employing involuntary confessions or testimony it knows to be false. All these rights, the Supreme Court has held, are indispensable to a fair trial.[4]

In addition, overcoming initial fears that to do so would make much of the Bill of Rights redundant, the Court has held that the Due Process Clause of the Fourteenth Amendment makes applicable to the states many of the procedural rights that the first eight amendments guarantee, in addition to due process, against the United States. As under the Fourth Amendment, the accused is protected against unreasonable searches and seizures; and in order to deter the violation of this right the state is forbidden to use illegally obtained evidence at trial. As under the Fifth Amendment, the accused may neither be required to give evidence against himself nor be tried or punished more than once for a single offense. As under the Sixth Amendment, he has the right to a jury trial, to confront the witnesses against him, and to the assistance of counsel—at state expense if necessary. As under the Eighth Amendment, he may not be subjected to punishments that are "cruel and unusual."[5]

All of this looks very civilized and proper. There is just one catch: relatively few persons charged with crimes are actually tried according to these exemplary standards. The typical procedure is for the defendant to waive his rights by pleading guilty in exchange for a lenient sentence and to receive no trial at all. One might have expected the Supreme Court to hold that a guilty plea induced by a promise of leniency was, like an involuntary out-of-court confession, ineffective. Defenders of the "plea bargaining" system argue that it saves the state money and analogize it to the settlement of civil suits; opponents argue that it punishes defendants for insisting on their constitutional right to a fair trial.[6] The Court has upheld it;[7] the brave guarantees of the Constitution do not reflect the reality of today's criminal process.

Not only in criminal proceedings, but in civil and administrative proceedings as well, due process requires fair procedure whenever the state deprives a person of "life, liberty, or property." As will appear later in this chapter, the Supreme Court has given the term "liberty" in these provisions a broad interpretation.[8] In recent years "property" too has been broadly construed to include many interests in such government benefits as public employment and welfare payments. It is no longer an objection that the state has no constitutional duty to hire secretaries or support the needy.[9] It is enough that the law gives persons who meet prescribed criteria a legal right or "entitlement" to receive the benefit in question; only when the law leaves the decision whether or not to grant a benefit to the discretion of the administering official can it be said that no property is involved.[10]

What sort of procedure due process requires in order to deprive a person of life, liberty, or property depends upon a balancing of opposing interests: How serious is the invasion of the affected private interest, how useful are the contested procedures, and how seriously do they burden the public interest?[11] In *Goldberg v. Kelly*, for example, where the termination of welfare benefits endangered a recipient's very survival, the Supreme Court demanded a prior administrative hearing similar to a judicial trial.[12] In *Goss v. Lopez*, on the other hand, where an allegedly misbehaving pupil faced only a brief suspension from school, it was enough that the principal orally informed him of the grounds for suspension and gave him the chance to respond on the spot.[13] Indeed, when an administrator promulgates general rules, due process has been held to impose no procedural restraints at all; the large number of people affected both makes the cost of formal proceedings prohibitive and strengthens the possibility that they can defend their interests by political means.[14]

Due process also plays a significant role as an instrument of federalism by helping to mark the boundaries between the powers of the individual states. Like the Full Faith and Credit Clause of article IV, due process forbids one state to meddle in the affairs of another. A state may not, for example, apply its own law to a dispute in whose

outcome it has no legitimate concern.[15] Similarly, due process limits
the geographical scope of state tax power and of state judicial process;
a person may be neither taxed by nor required to litigate in a state
with which he has no relevant connection.[16]

SUBSTANTIVE DUE PROCESS

In *Lochner v. New York*, decided in 1905, the state had forbidden
bakers to work their employees more than 60 hours a week.[17] In *Roe
v. Wade*, decided in 1973, the state had outlawed abortion.[18] The
Supreme Court declared both statutes unconstitutional: the one deprived the baker and the other the pregnant woman of liberty without due process of law.

The first decision is old, the second new; the first "conservative,"
the second "liberal." Yet both reflect the same basic constitutional
principle: that the Due Process Clauses invalidate unreasonable laws.

Dissenting Justices argued in both cases that the laws in question
were not unreasonable. The maximum-hour law, they contended,
protected bakery employees from exploitation and disease; the abortion law protected maternal health and the lives of unborn children.
Both were therefore reasonable means of achieving legitimate governmental ends, and thus both should have been upheld.[19]

Agreeing that the promotion of health was a legitimate goal, the
majority in *Lochner* argued that the maximum-hour law was an inappropriate means of attaining it. In contrast to mining, where a similar
statute had been upheld,[20] baking was in their opinion not a dangerous occupation. Protecting workers against economic exploitation,
they added, was not even a legitimate purpose: apart from protecting
the worker's health, the state had no interest in regulating the terms of
employment.

All the Justices professed to agree that the Due Process Clause prohibited only *unreasonable* laws, not unwise ones; the Court was not

entitled to substitute its judgment for that of the legislature. As the dissenters demonstrated, however, it was difficult to conclude that the limitation of bakers' hours was unreasonable. To begin with, studies cited by Justice John Harlan had found that baking was indeed dangerous; because of the constant heat and dust, he concluded, bakers "seldom live over their fiftieth year." Moreover, as Justice Oliver Wendell Holmes argued, reasonable people could also believe that even adult bakers needed protection against the superior bargaining power of their employers.

The law struck down in *Lochner* would clearly be upheld today. The decision itself was silently abandoned in 1917.[21] In 1937 the Court went further, overruling decisions that had struck down minimum-wage legislation as well.[22] Since that time, in fact, the Court has shown such extreme deference to legislative judgment in cases involving property or other economic interests that in these areas the concept of "substantive due process" on which *Lochner* was based has virtually disappeared.[23] A 1963 decision allowing a state to limit the business of "debt adjusting" to lawyers seemed to announce the death knell of the entire doctrine: "There was a time when the Due Process Clause was used by this Court to strike down laws which were thought unreasonable . . . . [That doctrine] has long been discarded. . . . It is now settled that States 'have power to legislate against what are found to be injurious practices in their internal commercial and business affairs, so long as their laws do not run afoul of some specific federal constitutional prohibition . . . .'"[24]

At the same time the Supreme Court was burying substantive due process in its original economic field, however, it began to employ the same concept as a device for applying the guarantees of the First Amendment to the states. That amendment itself, like the rest of the Bill of Rights, applies only to the federal government.[25] Freedom of speech, press, religion, and assembly, however, no less than freedom of contract, came within the "liberty" protected by the Due Process Clause of the Fourteenth Amendment, the Court concluded, because they were "fundamental."[26]

Moreover, the Court decided, First Amendment liberties enjoyed a "preferred position" entitling them to greater judicial protection than ordinary economic liberties. Legislation affecting economic interests would be upheld if the legislature had a "rational basis" for adopting it. "But freedoms of speech and of press, of assembly and of worship may not be infringed on such slender grounds. They are susceptible of restriction only to prevent grave and immediate danger to interests which the State may lawfully protect."[27]

Justice Felix Frankfurter protested in dissent that "[t]he Constitution does not give us greater veto power when dealing with one phase of 'liberty' than with another."[28] The majority, however, seemed to think the fact that freedoms such as speech and religion were specifically enumerated as against Congress entitled them to greater respect against the states than other liberties protected by the Due Process Clause.[29] *Roe v. Wade*, moreover, expanded the category of liberties entitled to special protection beyond those listed in other Bill of Rights provisions.

Like freedom of speech and religion, *Roe* concluded, and unlike the "liberty of contract" protected in *Lochner*, a woman's interest in having an abortion was "fundamental." A fundamental interest could be restricted only to promote a *compelling* governmental purpose, not a merely legitimate one; and the restriction must be "narrowly drawn to express only the legitimate state interests at stake." Judged by this exacting standard, the law challenged in *Roe* failed; a blanket prohibition of abortions not required to save the life of the mother was not a narrowly tailored means to a compelling governmental end.

The decisive difference between *Roe* and *Lochner*, in short, lies in the judges' willingness to scrutinize laws far more strictly when they restrict "fundamental" rights and in their current perception that the right to an abortion is more fundamental than liberty of contract. If reasonableness is the test, it is fair enough to say that more severe invasions of liberty require more compelling justification; but determining the relative importance of liberties that differ in kind rather than degree is a highly subjective process largely dependent upon the value systems of individual judges.

The first argument against both the *Lochner* and *Roe* decisions is therefore that the laws challenged in those cases were not unreasonable. But there are more basic objections.

First, there is historical evidence to suggest that the Supreme Court may have construed the term "liberty" in the Due Process Clauses more broadly than was originally intended. The origin of these provisions was the famous Magna Carta of 1215, which provided that no one should be "taken, imprisoned, disinherited, or put to death" except by the judgment of his peers or the law of the land. Magna Carta protected only freedom from *imprisonment*, not freedom in general; and due process grew up as a paraphrase of the Magna Carta provision.[30] The Supreme Court gave no reason for its conclusion that "liberty" in the Due Process Clauses meant more than the liberty protected by the provision from which they were derived.[31]

Second, the notion that the Due Process Clauses limit the *substantive* content of the law is difficult to reconcile with either the text or the history of those provisions. The words "due process" suggest only a suitable *procedure* for the deprivation of rights, not a prohibition on taking them away at all.[32] Justice Joseph Story defined due process in purely procedural terms in 1833 as a trial according to the "processes and proceedings" of the common law;[33] the Supreme Court gave no reason for its contrary conclusion.

Third, the derivation of the Due Process Clauses from Magna Carta suggests that they may not have been meant to limit legislative power in any way. "Due process of law," as noted, was originally synonymous with "the law of the land." These words suggest only that the executive and the courts must act *in accordance with law.* In England, where Parliamentary authority is unlimited, they clearly do not restrict legislative power. The Supreme Court supported its conclusion that the framers of the Constitution had departed from this settled understanding by arguing that otherwise the Due Process Clauses would be "of no avail."[34]

This argument is not convincing. That the state may deprive the individual of life, liberty, or property only on the basis of law is a barrier of first importance to arbitrary executive action and a hallmark of the historic transition to representative government. "With all its delays, defects, and inconveniences," wrote Justice Jackson in the steel-seizure case, "men have discovered no technique for long preserving free government except that the executive be under the law, and that the law be made by parliamentary deliberations."[35] The New Hampshire Supreme Court's 1817 explanation of a "law of the land" provision is equally persuasive as applied to due process today: "This clause was not intended to abrogate the power of the legislature, but to assert the right of every citizen to be secure from all arrests not warranted by law."[36]

Despite these difficulties, substantive due process has survived; to the surprise of many, a more conservative Court reaffirmed *Roe v. Wade* on the basis of precedent in 1992.[37] Like most provisions of the Bill of Rights, however, the Due Process Clauses merely forbid the government to "deprive" persons of their rights; they do not in general require affirmative government action to *protect* life, liberty, or property. Thus, for example, the Supreme Court has made clear that although the state may not forbid abortions it need not subsidize them, even for those who cannot afford to bear the cost themselves.[38] The history of these provisions lends force to the textual inference that they were meant to protect the individual from the state, not to require the state to provide her with social services or protect her from third parties.[39]

ALTERNATIVE THEORIES

Substantive due process, I have argued, rests on a shaky founda-
tion. Persons in positions of power, however, are naturally tempted to
find ways of correcting what they perceive as injustice; and it is not
surprising that judges have sought a general prohibition of unreasonable laws outside the due-process provisions as well.

Long before the adoption of the Fourteenth Amendment, for example, Justice Samuel Chase hinted that state authority might be limited by "the great first principles of the social compact" whether or not
they were embodied in the Constitution.[40] His colleague James Iredell
took issue with him on the spot: judicial authority to strike down laws
inconsistent with "natural justice" contradicted not only the principle
of democratic rule but all of English history and the idea of a written
Constitution too. It also appears to offend both the Tenth Amendment and the Supremacy Clause of article VI; for the former reserves
to the states all powers not forbidden by the Constitution itself, while
the latter makes constitutional acts of Congress the "law of the land."

Chase's suggestion of extraconstitutional limitations on government power has not survived. Later Justices, however, sought a hand-
hold for a general prohibition of unreasonable laws in the Fourteenth
Amendment provision forbidding any state to "abridge the privileges
or immunities of citizens of the United States." When Louisiana
granted a monopoly to a single slaughterhouse, for example, Justice
Joseph Bradley argued in dissent that it had abridged the "privilege"
of other butchers to practice their trade.[41]

The majority disagreed. The privileges "of citizens of the United
States," wrote Justice Samuel Miller, were those which the citizen enjoyed *by virtue of* United States citizenship—those conferred by other
provisions of federal law. The right to slaughter animals was based on
state law, not federal; and thus the Fourteenth Amendment did not
protect it.

Dissenting Justices predictably protested that the majority's interpretation left the clause without meaning: if it protected only rights that were already protected, there was no point in having the clause at all. Even on the Court's interpretation, however, the clause served the useful purpose of enabling Congress (under § 5 of the same amendment) to enact remedial measures to prevent state infringement of pre-existing federal rights; the dissenters' objections were overdrawn.

The words of the Privileges or Immunities Clause are ambiguous. The congressional debates on the provision, moreover, offer some support not only for both Miller's and Bradley's interpretations but for two others as well.

The sponsor of the amendment, for example, told the Senate that this clause would make the entire Bill of Rights applicable to the states. That no state should "abridge the privileges or immunities of citizens of the United States," in other words, meant that no state could infringe privileges like freedom of speech and of religion, which previously had been guaranteed only against the United States.[42] A number of Justices, so far always in dissent, have adopted this position.[43]

What most thoroughly pervades the debates, however, is the overriding intention of Congress to provide an unshakable constitutional basis for the Civil Rights Act of 1866, which had forbidden the states to deny blacks certain privileges or immunities enjoyed by whites—such as the right to contract or own property. The text of the Privileges or Immunities Clause was taken from article IV of the Constitution, which provided that "[t]he citizens of each state shall be entitled to all privileges and immunities of citizens in the several states." This provision forbade a state to discriminate against citizens of other states in distributing privileges or immunities;[44] the debates suggest that by employing similar language the framers of the Fourteenth Amendment may have meant to forbid a state to discriminate against its own black citizens as well.[45]

The Court has rejected not only these alternative theories but also Justice Bradley's notion that the Privileges or Immunities Clause pro-

vides protection against all laws invading fundamental rights. In recent years, however, a fourth hook has been brought forward on
which to hang a general judicial authority to invalidate unreasonable
laws. This is the Ninth Amendment, which provides that "[t]he enumeration in the Constitution, of certain rights, shall not be construed
to deny or disparage others retained by the people."

On its face this provision seems to imply that the people have
rights other than those listed in the Constitution. It does not, however, say that these unidentified rights are of constitutional rank, or
that they limit the powers given to government elsewhere in the same
document. The origin of the amendment, in fact, suggests a quite different purpose.

Opponents of the Bill of Rights had argued that the First Amendment's prohibition of laws abridging freedom of the press was unnecessary because nothing in the Constitution gave Congress authority
over the press to begin with. Indeed, Alexander Hamilton argued,
such a prohibition could be downright dangerous. Because there was
no point in limiting powers that did not exist, the amendment might
be taken to imply that Congress did have authority to regulate the
press so long as it did not abridge its freedom.

The purpose of the Ninth Amendment, according to its sponsor
James Madison, was to quiet these fears. The Bill of Rights, in other
words, was not to be taken to imply a broad interpretation of the
powers given Congress to limit the "rights" of the people.[46] This history suggests that, like the Tenth Amendment, the Ninth does not
limit the authority elsewhere given to the government; it is instructive
that so liberal a Justice as William O. Douglas concluded that it "obviously does not create federally enforceable rights."[47]

Despite its controversial pedigree, therefore, due process remains
the instrument by means of which the judges oversee the reasonableness of the laws. Although most recent substantive due-process
decisions have been "liberal," the juxtaposition of *Roe v. Wade* with

Lochner v. New York should put to rest any notion that substantive due process is good for liberal causes in general. Indeed the doctrine made its Supreme Court debut in the infamous *Dred Scott* decision as one basis for the indefensible holding that Congress had no power to forbid slavery in the territories.[48]

Justice Byron White put the point well in a 1986 opinion explaining the Court's refusal to protect sexual practices the law had long forbidden as immoral: "The Court is most vulnerable and comes nearest to illegitimacy when it deals with judge-made constitutional law having little or no cognizable roots in the language or design of the Constitution."[49]

6   *Equality*

T HE THIRTEENTH AMENDMENT, adopted at the end of the Civil
    War in 1865, abolished slavery. The former slaves continued to
suffer, however, from systematic official discrimination. Southern
states enacted so-called "Black Codes" denying them such privileges
as the right to contract, to vote, or to own land. Blacks were punished
more severely than whites who had committed similar offenses.
Often the states even refused to enforce their laws to protect blacks
from murder and theft.[1]

The central purpose of the Fourteenth and Fifteenth Amendments was to stamp out this discrimination. Two clauses of the Fourteenth have already been discussed. The present chapter deals principally with another: "[N]or shall any State deny to any person within
its jurisdiction the equal protection of the laws."

RACIAL DISCRIMINATION AND SEGREGATION

The language and history of the Equal Protection Clause suggest
that it may have been intended to ensure that states afforded blacks
the same protection against crimes that they afforded other citizens.[2]
After the Supreme Court concluded that the Privileges or Immunities Clause of the same amendment merely protected rights given by
other federal laws,[3] however, equal protection had to be construed
more broadly if the amendment's purpose of preventing state racial
discrimination was to be achieved at all. It was therefore no surprise
when the Supreme Court held in 1880 that the Equal Protection
Clause forbade a state to exclude blacks from serving on juries.[4]

Whether the amendment also forbade the mere *separation* of the
races was another story. When a state required separate railroad cars

for blacks and whites, for example, the Supreme Court in the well-known case of *Plessy v. Ferguson* in 1896 found no violation of the Constitution. The Fourteenth Amendment, the Court concluded, forbade only unequal treatment of the races; "separate" facilities for blacks and whites were permissible so long as they were "equal."[5]

Eventually the Supreme Court began to recognize that separate facilities for blacks were in fact often unequal. In 1938, for example, the Justices ordered a black applicant admitted to a "white" state university on the ground that the alternative of a state-financed education elsewhere was inferior.[6] In 1954, however, in *Brown v. Board of Education*, the Court took a giant step toward eliminating the principle of racial segregation itself. Black pupils knew that separate schools had been established for discriminatory reasons, wrote Chief Justice Earl Warren, and the resulting sense of inferiority impaired their ability to learn. Thus there were no "separate but equal" public schools: "Separate educational facilities are inherently unequal."[7]

Although the Justices in *Brown* had emphasized the particular effects of segregation on the educational process, later decisions extended the prohibition of racial separation to other facilities such as parks and restaurants without additional explanation.[8] A few years later, in striking down a statute forbidding interracial marriages, the Court enunciated a broader principle that put an end to the "separate but equal" thesis altogether: The Fourteenth Amendment not only required that blacks be treated as well as whites but also demanded "'the most rigid scrutiny'" of *any* "distinctions based on race."[9]

It was true that the law in question treated blacks and whites "equally" in the sense that *neither* could marry a person of another race. In another sense, however, members of both groups were subjected to significant disabilities on racial grounds; only a white man, for example, was forbidden to marry a black woman. The rights given by the Fourteenth Amendment, as the Court has said, are "personal rights." It is no solace to one who has been denied a right for reasons

of race to know that members of other races are denied other rights
of equal value. "Equal protection of the laws," as the Court said in another case, "is not achieved through indiscriminate imposition of in-
equalities."[10]

The authors of the Fourteenth Amendment might have been sur-
prised by this result. The general wording of the clause, however, suggests that they intended to leave the determination of what consti-
tuted "equal protection" to those who would interpret the provision
in the future. The conclusion that race is an impermissible ground of
official classification is entirely consistent with the language of the
clause; and it corresponds far better to the general concept of racial
equality than does the discredited doctrine of "separate but equal."[11]

Affirmative Action and De Facto Discrimination

The typical case of racial discrimination in this country involves
the disadvantageous treatment of blacks or other historically disfavored minorities. In recent years the converse question has come in-
creasingly to the fore: May the state afford such minorities *preferential* treatment?

It is clear that the immediate goal of the amendment was to end
official discrimination against blacks. The constitutional language,
however, is not so limited; the states are forbidden to deny "*any person*" equal protection of the laws. The text suggests that the framers
of the amendment drew from the tragic history of African-Americans
the refreshing lesson that *no one* should be disadvantaged on grounds
of race.

As early as 1880 the Supreme Court employed the analogy of a
hypothetical discrimination against whites to support its conclusion
that the Fourteenth Amendment forbade discrimination against
blacks: If a law "exclud[ed] all white men from jury service, . . . we
apprehend that no one would be heard to claim that it would not be

a denial to white men of the equal protection of the laws."[12] Nearly a hundred years later, in *Regents of the University of California v. Bakke*, the Court appeared to confirm this suggestion by declaring invalid a provision effectively requiring that at least 16% of the students in a state medical school be members of certain minorities.[13]

Four Justices, however, avoided the constitutional question, relying instead upon a federal statute forbidding racial discrimination. Four others, moreover, thought the provision should be sustained. Though "equal protection" demanded careful scrutiny of racial classifications, it did not outlaw them altogether. Laws disadvantaging whites, in their view, were easier to justify than those disadvantaging blacks, because whites were politically powerful and had not traditionally been victims of discrimination. The quota favoring minorities was thus permissible, they argued, because it was "substantially related to achievement" of the "important governmental objective" of remedying the effects of past discrimination against them. Justice Lewis Powell, who cast the deciding vote, agreed in principle that the state could favor minorities to some degree in the interest of diversifying the student body, concluding only that a rigid numerical quota was an unnecessarily burdensome means of achieving the state's legitimate goals.

Thus the *Bakke* decision did not condemn racial preferences entirely. Two years later, over only three dissents, the Court actually upheld a provision reserving "at least 10 per centum" of federal funds expended on local public-works projects for enterprises owned by "Negroes, Spanish-speaking, Orientals, Indians, Eskimos and Aleuts." Even a numerical quota, in the majority's view, was permissible where Congress had discovered a history of racial discrimination.[14]

There are several difficulties with this conclusion. As an original matter, the text of the amendment seems to suggest racial equality in all cases, not merely when Congress or the Court finds it appropriate.[15] Moreover, there was no proof in either of the cases just discussed that the individuals given preferential treatment had previously been victims of racial discrimination, or that those to whom they were preferred had caused or profited from their plight. Some blacks, in other words, were preferred because some whites had been favored in the past. The relationship between the wrong and the remedy was arguably too crude to withstand the strict test that the Justices themselves prescribed for the fit between racial classifications and the ends they were designed to achieve.

At the policy level, it is far from clear that the Court's conclusion that racial distinctions are sometimes permissible will really work in the long run to the benefit of those it was intended to help. Fifty years ago this same principle led the Supreme Court to affirm the deplorable decision to drive American citizens of Japanese descent from their homes on the West Coast out of fear that they might be disloyal during the war with Japan.[16] An argument can be made that politically powerless minorities are most secure if racial classifications are forbidden entirely.[17]

As Presidents Reagan and Bush appointed additional conservative Justices, the Court's support for preferences for members of racial minorities began to erode. In *Richmond County v. J. A. Croson Co.*, in 1989, the Court made clear that states could not set aside construction jobs for members of minority groups without proof of prior discrimination.[18] In *Adarand Constructors v. Peña*, in 1995, by a vote of 5-4, it squarely held that distinctions that favored racial minorities were subject to the same strict scrutiny as those that disadvantaged them: "[A]ll racial classifications, imposed by whatever federal, state, or local government actor, . . . are constitutional only if they are narrowly tailored measures that further compelling governmental interests."[19]

The Court has thus left a narrow window of opportunity for racial distinctions carefully crafted to remedy the effects of past discrimination. Litigants have so far failed to persuade the Justices, however, to employ the Equal Protection Clause to remedy what is sometimes called de facto segregation or discrimination.

As a result of the Supreme Court's decision that white and black pupils could not be assigned to separate schools on the basis of race, many schools have been racially integrated. Half a century later, however, there remain many other schools in which the students are essentially all black or all white. Today this result is commonly traceable to the fact that blacks and whites tend to live in different neighborhoods rather than to any official decision to separate pupils according to race.

Laws requiring children to attend school in their own neighborhoods obviously serve legitimate interests in efficiency. Should they nevertheless be condemned as racially discriminatory because they have the *effect* of separating pupils of different races? What the Constitution forbids, the Court has concluded, is differential treatment *on grounds of race*; it does not require affirmative efforts to achieve racial balance. Thus, for example, so far as the Constitution is concerned, a police department not motivated by racial bias may set identical standards for black and white job applicants, even if a disproportionate number of blacks prove unable to meet them.[20] The Constitution merely protects the individual against wrongful action by government; the state need not eliminate de facto differences that it did not cause.[21]

Nonracial Classifications

The central purpose of the Fourteenth Amendment, as noted, was to eliminate official race discrimination. The text, however, appears to state a more general principle of equality: No state shall "deny to any person . . . the equal protection of the laws." Consequently, despite early suggestions to the contrary,[22] the Supreme Court has consistently held that the Equal Protection Clause forbids discrimination on grounds other than race as well.

This historically debatable conclusion created serious difficulties of interpretation. So long as the provision was limited to race, it could be taken to require unqualified equality, as its terms suggest. Common sense, however, precludes the conclusion that the authors of the amendment meant to require that everyone be treated equally under all conditions—that blind three-year olds be issued drivers' licenses, for example, or that murderers go unpunished. Equal protection accordingly came to mean equal treatment of persons "similarly situated"; all persons must be treated equally if they should be.

In most equal-protection cases, as in substantive due process cases not involving "fundamental" rights, the standard of review is extremely deferential; most distinctions will be upheld if there is a "rational basis" for them. So far as the Constitution is concerned, for example, a state may require all police officers to retire at the age of fifty, though it is likely that some of them are still fit. It is enough that older persons as a rule are less equal to the substantial physical demands of the job.[23]

Such a crude relationship between a legislative goal and the means chosen for attaining it, however, is not always permitted. That police officers should be well educated as well as in good physical condition is, as we have seen, a legitimate end.[24] It may not be pursued, however, by making only whites eligible to be officers, even if experience shows that whites on the average have been better educated than blacks. Racial distinctions may not be all the Equal Protection Clause forbids, but they lie at its heart. Race is a "suspect" basis of classification because it is an immutable characteristic that is usually irrelevant to any legitimate governmental purpose and that has frequently been misused. Racial classifications, therefore, like measures impinging on interests deemed "fundamental" under the Due Process Clauses, must generally be "justified by a *compelling* governmental interest and must be *'necessary'*" to its accomplishment.[25]

Distinctions respecting "fundamental" rights are subject to strict scrutiny under the Equal Protection Clause as well. In *Reynolds v. Sims*, for example, the Court required that seats in state legislatures be apportioned equally according to population after concluding that voting rights were fundamental and that there was no compelling reason to give some voters more electoral power than others.[26]

Classifications on the basis of gender are also subject to heightened scrutiny; most recently the Court has said they require an "exceedingly persuasive justification."[27] "[T]hus far," the Court noted in the opinion just quoted, distinctions between men and women have not been treated with quite the same degree of suspicion as those based on race. A mere "rational basis," however, will not suffice; the state must show "at least" that the distinction is "substantially related" to "important governmental objectives."

Thus in contrast to a distinction based on age, for example, the fact that more young men than young women drive while drunk was held not to justify setting the drinking age higher for men than for women.[28] In contrast to a distinction based on race, on the other hand, the Court upheld a law requiring only men to register for a possible military draft on the ground that only men could be ordered into battle—although physical strength, as the dissenters pointed out, was neither confined to males nor necessary for dropping bombs, and although women were in demand for noncombatant military duties.[29] But that was in 1981; it is not certain the case would be decided the same way today.

The fact that most sex classifications have lately been struck down on the basis of equal protection may well have dampened enthusiasm for efforts to adopt an "Equal Rights Amendment" explicitly pro-

hibiting discrimination on grounds of sex.[30] Advocates of this proposal emphatically denied that it would make gender constitutionally
irrelevant in all cases, so as to permit marriages, for example, between
two women. Thus the probable effect of the proposed amendment
would have been to require a "compelling" rather than a merely "important" interest to support gender as well as race distinctions.
Whether or not this subtle difference alone would justify the dramatic step of amending the Constitution, however, the proposed
amendment would have symbolic value in formally committing the
nation to a basic principle of justice and protect against possible second thoughts about the present protective interpretation of the Fourteenth Amendment.

STATE ACTION

The Equal Protection Clause, like the other prohibitions of the
Fourteenth Amendment, is directed toward the states. "No state" may
abridge the privileges or immunities of United States citizens, deprive
persons of life, liberty, or property without due process of law, or deny
anyone equal protection of the laws. This means both that state legislatures may not pass unequal laws[31] and that state laws must be
equally executed or applied. The courts may not exclude blacks from
jury duty;[32] the executive may not deny permits to all Chinese who
wish to operate laundries.[33]

Only the *states*, however, are forbidden to discriminate. The plain
text of the amendment makes this clear, as do the spirit and history
of the whole Constitution. Almost without exception, the Constitution regulates relations between the individual and government, not
among citizens themselves.[34]

Accordingly, in the *Civil Rights Cases* in 1883, the Supreme Court
concluded that § 5 of the Fourteenth Amendment gave Congress no
authority to outlaw racial discrimination in private restaurants, ho-

tels, or theaters.[35] Section 5 empowers Congress to enact only legisla-tion "to enforce . . . the provisions" of the amendment itself; and nothing in the amendment forbade purely private discrimination.

Today Congress may forbid much private discrimination on the basis of other constitutional authority.[36] It remains true, however, that the Fourteenth Amendment binds only the state and not the in-dividual citizen. What prohibitions of private discrimination we have—and we now have an impressive array of them at both state and federal levels—we owe to the lawmakers, not to the Constitu-tion itself.

It is not always easy to decide, however, whether the state is re-sponsible for a particular instance of discrimination. In the famous case of *Shelley v. Kraemer*, for example, the Supreme Court held that a state court could not enforce a restrictive covenant in a private deed forbidding sale of a lot to blacks.[37] The action of the court, as the Jus-tices observed, was that of the state for purposes of the Equal Protec-tion Clause.

It was not the state, however, that had *discriminated*; state law provided in racially neutral terms for the enforcement of private agreements without regard to their content. The logic of the decision suggests that the police may not assist a householder motivated by racial prejudice in removing an unwanted person from his premises. Such a result would turn the Fourteenth Amendment, despite its ex-plicit limitation to state action, into a potent restriction on private autonomy.

The Supreme Court has refused to carry its logic this far. State is-suance of a permit for a private club, for example, has been held in-sufficient to make the state responsible for the club's discriminatory acts.[38] Racial discrimination in a private restaurant on state land, on the other hand, has been attributed to the state itself.[39] The decisions are numerous, the distinctions narrow; generalizations as to what of-

ficial involvement renders the state responsible for private discrimination are dangerous.[40]

It is also noteworthy that—unlike the Due Process Clauses and
the Fifteenth Amendment—the Equal Protection Clause applies only
to the states and not to the United States. This omission reflects the
fact that the principal impetus for the adoption of the amendment
was racial discrimination by the states, not by the federal government.

Unfortunately, however, Congress itself has not always been immune to the corrosive influence of racism. As late as 1954, at the same
time the Justices invalidated school segregation in the states, they
were asked to determine the constitutionality of a similar requirement
enacted by Congress for the District of Columbia. Although the
Equal Protection Clause was inapplicable, the Court held the law unconstitutional. Ever since *Lochner v. New York*, arbitrary laws had
been held to deprive individuals of liberty without due process of law;
and there was no rational basis for excluding black pupils from white
schools.[41]

As a matter of morality or policy, this result was certainly to be ap-
plauded. As a matter of constitutional law, however, it poses serious
problems. To begin with, it remains difficult to reconcile the concept
of "substantive due process" with either the text or the history of the
constitutional provision, and by 1954, apart from serving as a vehicle
for applying the Bill of Rights to the states, the doctrine itself had virtually disappeared.[42] More specifically, there is a Due Process Clause
in the Fourteenth Amendment as well as in the Fifth; the explicit
Equal Protection Clause would be entirely superfluous if another
clause of the same amendment already forbade the states to deny
equal protection.[43] Finally, the amendment protects only "life, liberty,
or property" against deprivation without due process of law. The
Constitution does not require the government to provide anyone
with an education, and the statute could hardly be said to deprive per-

sons of the very interest it created. It is thus difficult to see how the exclusion of black children from white schools by statute deprived them of either liberty or property as the Supreme Court has defined those terms.[44]

The Court revealed the true basis for its decision at the end of its opinion: "In view of our decision that the Constitution prohibits the states from maintaining racially segregated public schools, it would be unthinkable that the same Constitution would impose a lesser duty on the Federal Government." It may have been "unthinkable," but unfortunately it was true. When the Constitution proves deficient, the proper course is to amend it by the procedure prescribed in article V.

THE RIGHT TO VOTE

The Fourteenth Amendment punished states that denied blacks the right to vote by a corresponding reduction in their seats in the House of Representatives. Even the supporters of that amendment emphasized, however, that despite its broad terminology it did not forbid the states to deny voting rights on racial grounds.[45] This was rather the task of the Fifteenth Amendment, adopted in 1870: "The right of citizens of the United States to vote shall not be denied or abridged by the United States or by any State on account of race, color, or previous condition of servitude."

The Nineteenth and Twenty-sixth Amendments extended voting rights to women and to eighteen-year olds, and their enforcement was quick and painless. The Fifteenth Amendment, on the other hand, encountered stubborn resistance from the beginning, and it took a hundred years before blacks everywhere enjoyed the voting rights the Constitution assured them.

One of the cruder methods of circumventing the Fifteenth Amendment was the "grandfather clause." While prescribing voter qualifications that many blacks could not meet, Oklahoma exempted those applicants who (or whose ancestors) had been entitled to vote before the amendment was adopted. This exemption, needless to say, applied only to whites. Unable to find any conceivable purpose for such a provision other than forbidden race discrimination, the Supreme Court struck it down. That, however, was in 1915—nearly 50 years after the amendment had guaranteed blacks the right to vote.[46]

A second means of evasion was the white primary. Texas permitted black citizens to take part in the general election. Blacks were excluded, however, from the *primary* elections in which the political parties chose their candidates. In Texas, as in other Southern states at the time, there was essentially only one party; the Democratic nomination was tantamount to election. The practical result was that blacks had virtually no say in the choice of those who governed them.

To the extent that the state was responsible for the exclusion of blacks from party primaries, the Court had little difficulty in finding it unconstitutional. Whether or not the "right . . . to vote" protected by the Fifteenth Amendment extended to party primaries, a law excluding blacks from primaries denied them, in the Court's view, equal protection of the laws.[47]

After these decisions, the state left it entirely to the party to decide who could vote in their primaries. As expected, the party said whites only. At first the Supreme Court threw up its hands: what a political party decided could not be unconstitutional, because the Constitution limited only the states.[48]

In the 1940s, however, the Court began to perceive that there were occasions on which nominally private parties effectively were in the position of states and thus should be held to the same standards. The most obvious case was that of a company town, in which a private corporation performed all the functions usually carried out by municipal government. With good reason the Justices concluded that the corporation was in effect the "state" for purposes of the Fourteenth Amendment.[49] It required only a small step further to hold that a political party was likewise to be treated as the "state" when it conducted the election that practically determined who would hold public office.[50]

The grandfather clause and the white primary did not exhaust the arsenal of devices for denying blacks the right to vote. Limiting the vote to persons who had paid a poll tax, for example, effectively excluded more blacks than whites, because blacks were less affluent on the average. This requirement was harder to strike down than the grandfather clause; since it did help to collect revenue, it could hardly be said to serve no legitimate purpose at all. Because voting was a "fundamental" right, however, it could not be abridged without a compelling reason; and that a person was too poor to afford a poll tax, the Court concluded, was not a compelling reason for denying him the right to vote.[51]

Literacy tests, on the other hand, served a much more important purpose, for persons who cannot read are clearly at a disadvantage in understanding the political controversies the voters are expected to resolve. Consequently the Supreme Court felt constrained to uphold laws requiring that voters know how to read and write, despite the strong suspicion that their hidden purpose as well as their effect was to disenfranchise as many blacks as possible.[52] In 1970, however, because literacy tests had so often been applied discriminatorily, Congress outlawed them entirely. The Supreme Court, fairly enough, upheld this prohibition as a permissible means of enforcing the Fifteenth Amendment.[53]

Because some states had been so ingenious in devising new ways of evading the Fifteenth Amendment, Congress also provided that *no* new election law should take effect in an area with a history of voting discrimination until it was approved either by the Department of Justice or by a federal court. This unique limitation of state autonomy was also approved in 1966 as an appropriate means of finally effectuating the constitutional command.[54]

Thus it took virtually an entire century before the voting rights guaranteed blacks in 1870 became a reality. This is hardly a chapter of constitutional history to which one can point with pride. It is, however, a sobering reminder of the limited power of a well-intentioned Constitution.

7   *Freedom of Speech and of the Press*

T HE FIRST AMENDMENT provides that "Congress shall make no law . . . abridging the freedom of speech, or of the press." Since at least the 1930s the states have been under a similar restriction, for according to the Supreme Court freedom of expression is an element of the "liberty" protected by the Fourteenth Amendment against state deprivation without due process of law.[1]

"Those who won our independence," wrote the great Justice Louis Brandeis in 1927, "believed that the final end of the state was to make men free to develop their faculties; and that in its government the deliberative forces should prevail over the arbitrary. They valued liberty both as an end and as a means. . . . They believed that freedom to think as you will and to speak as you think are means indispensable to political truth; that without free speech and assembly discussion would be futile; that with them, discussion affords ordinarily adequate protection against the dissemination of noxious doctrine; that the greatest menace to freedom is an inert people; that public discussion is a political duty; and that this should be a fundamental principle of the American government. . . . Believing in the power of reason as applied through public discussion, they eschewed silence coerced by law[;] . . . they amended the Constitution so that free speech and assembly should be guaranteed."[2]

This does not mean that one may say whatever one pleases whenever, wherever, and however one chooses. The amendment's explicit language ("Congress shall make *no law*") does make clear that freedom of speech or of the press may never be abridged. What is protected against abridgment, however, is not speech itself but the *freedom* of speech; the problem is to determine the extent of that freedom.

Freedom to speak was certainly not absolute at the time the Constitution was adopted. Defamation, among other things, was traditionally prohibited. Nor does it seem likely that the framers of the amendment meant to protect such speech as incitement to murder, false advertising, or, as Justice Oliver Wendell Holmes once famously remarked, the false cry of "Fire!" in a crowded theater.[3]

Freedom of the press in England had meant only freedom from "previous restraints" such as laws requiring approval of books before publication.[4] The special vice of such a requirement is that even publications that are *not* prohibited are suppressed until licensing proceedings are concluded. Ordinary criminal laws, by contrast, permit one to publish without prior approval and defend on the ground that the publication was not forbidden.

For this reason previous restraints have always been especially difficult to justify. Court orders forbidding publication, for example, operate as previous restraints because the integrity of the judicial process requires that they be obeyed even if erroneous until set aside on appeal. Injunctions against publishing defamatory newspapers or confidential government files have accordingly been held unconstitutional.[5]

Justice Holmes's initial suggestion that the speech and press clauses prohibited *only* previous restraints,[6] however, has not prevailed. On the one hand, even as it condemned most such restraints, the Court recognized that an overpowering interest might occasionally require them: "No one would question but that a government might prevent . . . the publication of the sailing dates of transports or the number and location of troops."[7] On the other hand, as an influential commentator had argued as early as 1868, freedom of speech would poorly serve either the individual interest in self-expression or society's interest in a well-informed public if a speaker could always be punished once he had finished speaking.[8]

For these reasons the Supreme Court has taken as its standard for applying the speech and press guarantees not history but once again a balance of opposing interests. Behind the varying formulations for evaluating particular kinds of restraints lies a common inquiry: How seriously does the restriction limit communication, and how strong is society's interest in doing so?

In applying this criterion, the judges tend to be far less deferential to other branches than they often are in due-process or equal-protection cases.[9] Like racial equality and abortion rights, the "fundamental" interests protected by the First Amendment may commonly be restricted only to serve "compelling" governmental interests.[10]

CONTENT REGULATION

In applying the speech and press provisions, the Supreme Court distinguishes sharply between those regulations that limit the *content* of a statement or publication and those that neutrally limit the *time, place, or manner* of expression. A content limitation is especially difficult to justify because its impact on communication is especially grave: certain messages are placed at a competitive disadvantage, and in extreme cases they may not be conveyed at all.

In the famous 1919 case of *Schenck v. United States*,[11] for example, the defendant had been convicted of conspiracy to obstruct the recruitment of troops on the basis of a circular urging draftees to assert their right to oppose conscription. It was the message itself that the government sought to suppress; the interference with Schenck's interest in conveying it was severe. The public interest in suppressing that message, on the other hand, was also considerable. The government was protecting itself against the possible commission of a crime—the illegal refusal of draftees to serve. That crime, moreover, was one that in some circumstances could seriously threaten the national security.

In order to reconcile these competing interests to the extent possible, Holmes enunciated the familiar "clear and present danger" test:

The "question in every case is whether the words used are used in such circumstances and are of such a nature as to create a clear and present danger that they will bring about the substantive evils that Congress has a right to prevent."[12] This test was easily met in *Schenck*; there was an obvious and immediate risk that the offending circular might persuade draftees to refuse to serve.

Not all decisions upholding restrictions of this nature, however, appeared to satisfy Holmes's criteria. In 1951, in *Dennis v. United States*, a divided Court affirmed the conviction of leading members of the Communist Party for conspiring to overthrow the government by force and violence, although the projected coup lay in the distant and indefinite future. "Obviously," wrote Chief Justice Fred Vinson for four Justices, "the words cannot mean that before the government may act, it must wait until the putsch is about to be executed . . . ."[13] In other words, if the danger was grave enough, it did not have to be either clear or present.

Other decisions suggested that the clear and present danger test itself was insufficient to protect legitimate interests in expression. The Socialist leader Eugene Debs, for example, was punished for making a speech criticizing American participation in the First World War and praising persons who had been convicted of obstructing the draft.[14] As the Court noted, Debs's words, like Schenck's, might well have led to illegal draft evasion. The difficulty was that this was true of *all* criticism of the war effort. The clear and present danger test thus endangered the political debate whose protection lay at the heart of the First Amendment.[15]

In recognition of this danger, the Supreme Court in *Brandenburg v. Ohio* announced a significantly more protective standard. "The constitutional guarantees of free speech and free press," the Court declared, "do not permit a State to forbid or proscribe advocacy of the use of force or of law violation except where such advocacy is directed to inciting or producing imminent lawless action and is likely to incite or produce [it]."[16] I may not urge others to burn down the city hall. I may argue, however, that we would be better off without city government; in the interest of public debate, a free society must accept the risk that such an argument might lead to the commission of crime.

The extent to which this toleration of dangerous and unpalatable ideas is carried was illustrated by a 1978 state-court decision recognizing the right of members of the American Nazi Party to demonstrate with uniform and swastika in a predominantly Jewish neighborhood.[17] "The fitting remedy for evil counsels," as Justice Brandeis had said fifty years earlier, "is good ones. . . . If there be time to expose through discussion the falsehood and fallacies, to avert the evil by the processes of education, the remedy to be applied is more speech, not enforced silence."[18] Even those who would destroy our free society may propagate their views so long as they do not incite to immediate lawless action.

In the interest of open discussion of public issues, the Supreme Court has held that the First Amendment limits even the traditional right to recover damages for defamation. As Justice William Brennan wrote in denying a police commissioner compensation for an advertisement criticizing his department, the risk of paying damages to every official implicitly maligned by criticism of government could significantly dampen expression that lay at the very heart of the First Amendment's protection. Thus a public official can collect damages for injury to his reputation only if the statement is known to be false or is made with reckless disregard for its truth or falsity.[19]

Indirect restrictions of First Amendment freedoms are also forbidden. During the 1950s, for example, the Court held that Alabama could not compel the National Association for the Advancement of Colored People to disclose the names of its members. In the unfortunate climate then and there prevailing, wrote Justice John M. Harlan, the exposure of members of that organization could subject them to reprisals and discourage others from exercising their constitutional freedom.[20]

Legislative investigations into allegedly subversive activities pose similar problems. In the 1950s the Supreme Court tended to find compelling reasons of national security to justify the adverse effects of such investigations on protected freedoms. Subsequent decisions, however, have tended in the opposite direction.[21]

A final example is *Elrod v. Burns*, which held that a Democratic sheriff could not discharge Republican subordinates on political grounds. It was true, as Justice Holmes had observed many years earlier, that no one had a constitutional right to be a policeman. The risk of a political discharge, however, like the risk of exposure in the NAACP case, might well discourage policemen from protected political activity.[22] This does not mean that dangerous revolutionaries must be given access to state secrets; the balance of interests may be different when the impact on freedom of expression is indirect. If the purposes of the Constitution are to be attained, however, it is important that First Amendment freedoms be protected against indirect as well as direct limitation.

The First Amendment protects not only purely political speech but also works of art such as novels and motion pictures. That which entertains may also inform; even assuming that political speech lies at the heart of the amendment, the Court is unwilling to determine on a case-by-case basis which works of art lack political value.[23] Obscenity, however, narrowly defined to reflect the Court's perception that it is essentially without redeeming social value, remains without constitutional protection.[24]

Initially the Court took the view that purely "commercial" speech such as advertising was also unprotected.[25] In 1976, however, the Justices changed their minds. "Society," Justice Harry Blackmun wrote, "also may have a strong interest in the free flow of commercial information."[26] Apart from false advertising and incitement to illegal acts, a restriction on advertising will be upheld only if it "directly advances" a "substantial" governmental interest and is not unreasonably intrusive.[27]

TIME, PLACE, AND MANNER REGULATIONS

The categories of speech that may be forbidden altogether because of their content, therefore, are rare. Neutral regulations limiting the time, place, or manner of expression without regard to content, in contrast, are much easier to justify. On one side of the balance, such a regulation often interferes less with communication, since it leaves the speaker free to deliver the same message at another time or place or in another manner. On the other side, there are often compelling reasons to limit the time, place, or manner of communication.

I have no right, for example, to speak in your house without your permission; for you have an overriding interest in not being disturbed. I may not give speeches in the middle of the street without a permit, because the free flow of traffic takes priority.[28] On similar grounds the Supreme Court has held that a city may limit the use of loudspeakers[29] and restrict charitable solicitations in municipal airports.[30]

There are similar decisions upholding limitations on *symbolic* expression. Because draft cards might prove useful if it became necessary to call up additional troops, the Court held Congress could forbid burning them even to express opposition to the draft.[31] Similarly, even as a protest on behalf of the homeless, one may not sleep in a park contrary to regulations designed to protect conventional park uses.[32]

Cases such as these also pose the fundamental question whether such activities as sleeping and card-burning can properly be regarded as "speech" at all within the meaning of the First Amendment. On occasion the Supreme Court has expressed doubts on this score.[33] On the other hand, the Justices had no trouble in concluding, over half a century ago, that the display of a red flag was protected expression.[34] In light of the purposes of the amendment, an argument can be made that *any* act intended to convey information or ideas should qualify as "speech." As the draft-card case shows, this conclusion would by no means rule out the possibility that a particular means of communication might be prohibited on the basis of some overriding governmental concern.

It goes without saying that there are limits on the government's power to limit even the time, place, or manner of expression. The Court quite properly held the interest in clean streets insufficient to justify a flat ban on the distribution of handbills.[35] The ever-present risk of violence cannot support a prohibition of all mass demonstrations.[36] Even in passing on time, place, and manner regulations the Court must balance opposing interests, although it scrutinizes such regulations less strictly in the main: How important is it to speak at this particular time and place and in this particular manner, and how pressing are the countervailing interests of the state?

Even in enacting time, place, and manner regulations, moreover, the state may seldom discriminate according to the content of a speaker's message. Perhaps a state could prohibit *all* demonstrations in the vicinity of schools, in order to protect pupils from distraction and teachers from possible intimidation.[37] It is nevertheless clear that the state may not make an exception from such a prohibition for school-board employees involved in a labor dispute.[38] For one thing, such an exception suggests that the asserted interest in forbidding demonstrations may not be so compelling after all. More important, every preference of one side of a debate over another distorts the market of ideas that it was the central purpose of the First Amendment to foster.[39] Not even relatively innocuous time, place, and manner regulations may apply only to Republicans.[40]

Content distinctions are of two kinds, and they are treated somewhat differently for First Amendment purposes. *Viewpoint* discrimination is almost never allowed; unless the government itself is speaking, it may seldom take sides in a particular dispute.[41] *Subject-matter* discrimination is less suspect, for it bears equally on both sides, and it is less certain to be held invalid. Thus, for example, the government may limit political speech on military bases in order to reinforce the "tradition of a politically neutral military establishment"[42] and forbid the distribution of campaign literature in polling places to protect voters from intimidation and fraud.[43]

Finally, both to guard against possible discriminatory application and to help ensure that limitations of the fundamental right of expression reflect the will of the people, the Supreme Court has been especially insistent in speech cases that legislative discretion may not be delegated. Although the legislature may forbid street demonstrations without permits, it may not leave the determination of which demonstrations to permit to unguided administrative discretion. The lawmakers themselves must prescribe neutral, binding, and acceptable standards.[44]

Freedom of expression is thus certainly not absolute in the United States. Limitations discriminating on the basis of content, however, are especially difficult to justify, because they so severely restrict both private and public interests in communication. Even neutral time, place, and manner regulations, moreover, are subject to serious scrutiny to ensure that they limit the dissemination of information or opinion no more than is necessary to protect important governmental interests.

This broad protection of speech and press freedoms is one of the proudest accomplishments of the Constitution.

8   *Church and State*

THE FIRST AMENDMENT contains two provisions regarding the relations between church and state. "Congress shall make no law" either "respecting an establishment of religion" or "prohibiting the free exercise thereof."

Literally, like other First Amendment provisions, both clauses limit only Congress. The Supreme Court has held, however, that other branches of the federal government also lack power to infringe the rights the amendment protects.[1] Moreover, like the same amendment's guarantees of freedom of expression, the religion clauses have been held applicable to the states as well by virtue of the Fourteenth Amendment's Due Process Clause—even though that clause protects only "life, liberty, [and] property," and the Establishment Clause is not phrased in comparable terms.[2]

Both religion clauses pose difficult interpretive problems. In light of some of the decisions, indeed, it is difficult to reconcile the two provisions with each other; for in some cases one seems to require what the other forbids.

THE FREE EXERCISE OF RELIGION

Some applications of the Free Exercise Clause are obvious. Government may not forbid religious services generally or punish people for holding particular religious beliefs. It may not exclude members of a particular religious community from public service, for such disqualification would indirectly limit religious freedom.[3] Discrimination against dissenting denominations was the central evil the Free Exercise Clause was designed to prevent.[4]

Nor may a state exclude from public service persons who do not believe in God. Although the clause speaks only of the free exercise of "religion," its purpose was to establish a general freedom of conscience; and thus it also protects the right to have no religion at all.[5] The Free Exercise Clause reflects the lesson of the religious wars that racked Europe after the Reformation: without religious toleration there can be no civil peace.

Like freedom of expression, however, freedom of religion is not absolute.[6] Even religious conviction cannot justify mutilating women or sacrificing children. This is not to say the amendment protects only belief and not action; the text expressly guarantees the free *exercise* of religion. As the product of a campaign for religious equality, however, the Free Exercise Clause need not be read to create religious exceptions to general regulations serving legitimate secular goals.[7]

Thus the Supreme Court in 1879 held that Congress could forbid polygamy even among Mormons, for whom it was a religious duty.[8] An exception for Mormons, the Justices observed, would not only undermine the public interests underlying the law; it would also give Mormons special privileges solely because of their religion. Similarly, the First Amendment does not exempt conscientious objectors from college military training, Sabbatarians from laws limiting Sunday employment, or soldiers who wear religious caps from military dress regulations.[9] The principle of the First Amendment, these decisions suggest, is neutrality: no one may be either favored or disfavored on religious grounds.

Other decisions, however, cannot be reconciled with the neutrality principle. In sharp contrast to the Sunday-law case, for example, the Supreme Court held in *Sherbert v. Verner* that a state could not deny unemployment compensation to an applicant who refused for religious reasons to work on Saturday.[10] Still more strikingly, in *Wisconsin v. Yoder* the Court held that a child could not be required to attend high school against his religious principles.[11] In these cases the Justices interpreted the Free Exercise Clause to require not neutrality but—like the speech and press clauses of the same amendment—a balancing of opposing interests: How serious is the incursion on religious freedom, and how weighty is the state's countervailing interest?

The Supreme Court confronted these divergent lines of authority in the important case of *Employment Division v. Smith* in 1990.[12] The question was whether the Free Exercise Clause required Oregon to make an exception from its drug laws for Native Americans who used peyote for religious purposes. The answer was no. Writing for a bare majority of five judges, Justice Antonin Scalia explained away contrary precedents such as *Sherbert* and *Yoder*, concluding that the Court had "never held that an individual's religious beliefs excuse him from compliance with an otherwise valid law prohibiting conduct that the State is free to regulate." That was not true, but his argument on the merits was arresting: "a private right to ignore generally applicable laws" was "a constitutional anomaly."

Justice Sandra Day O'Connor agreed that religious peyote users were not entitled to an exemption, but she rejected Justice Scalia's analysis. To punish religiously motivated conduct obviously burdened the free exercise of religion. By analogy to free-speech cases, she argued, that should be permitted only when the law was narrowly tailored to promote a compelling state interest; and all the prior decisions were consistent with this test. Justice O'Connor herself found that the state had a compelling interest in suppressing the religious use of peyote; three other dissenters who agreed with her approach did not.

Congress reacted to the *Smith* decision by adopting the Religious Freedom Restoration Act, which attempted to enact Justice O'Connor's dissenting position into law: "Government may substantially burden a person's exercise of religion only if it demonstrates that application of the burden to the person (1) is in furtherance of a compelling governmental interest; and (2) is the least restrictive means of furthering that compelling governmental interest." The Supreme

Court, without dissent on this point, held the statute unconstitutional on the convincing ground that Congress cannot tell the Court how to interpret the Constitution.[13] Justice O'Connor, however, reaffirmed her view that *Smith* had been wrongly decided and her determination to reexamine the question in an appropriate case. We have not heard the last of the question whether the Free Exercise Clause requires religious exemptions from generally applicable laws.

THE ESTABLISHMENT OF RELIGION

In England there is, and in some colonies there was, an "established" church—an official, state-supported and state-regulated religion. There were at least two objections to this system. One denomination was preferred over others; and at the same time it was dependent upon the state.

The most obvious effect of the Establishment Clause was to preclude the creation of a national church, and the Fourteenth Amendment extended this prohibition to the states.[14] The text of the amendment ("no law *respecting* an establishment of religion"), however, suggests that the prohibition extends beyond this paradigm case. Indeed *all* preferences for particular religions implicate the evils that gave rise to the clause and therefore are likewise barred. The Establishment and Free Exercise Clauses can thus be viewed essentially as two sides of the same coin. The one forbids discrimination against a particular religion, the other forbids discrimination in its favor; for to favor one is to disadvantage all others.

Some have argued that preventing such preferential treatment was the sole office of the Establishment Clause. The same Congress that proposed the First Amendment voted to spend federal funds to employ a chaplain, and Justice Joseph Story, construing a similar provision of the Virginia constitution in 1815, suggested that an impartial subsidy of *all* religions would be permissible.[15] Unlike the establishment of a particular denomination, a general subsidy would neither disturb the natural balance among competing creeds nor be likely in most cases to entangle the state in sectarian affairs.

Nevertheless it is clear today that even an impartial subsidy of religion as such would be held invalid. What the clause forbids is the establishment not of *a* religion, but "*of religion*" in general. History furnishes impressive evidence that this choice of words was deliberate. Shortly before drafting the amendment itself, James Madison had objected to a general religious subsidy on the convincing ground, among others, that exacting money from taxpayers for religious purposes infringed their freedom of conscience. The Supreme Court has taken this remonstrance as a guide to the meaning of the Establishment Clause.[16]

Thus once again the Free Exercise and Establishment Clauses are complementary: The one forbids discrimination against those who have no religion, the other forbids preferences for those who have. The Court's well-known decisions forbidding state sponsorship of prayers in public schools[17] demonstrate that this principle extends beyond the money subsidies that Madison explicitly condemned. The Justices in these cases relied neither on the risk that the prayers might be more congenial to some denominations than to others, nor on the fact that the teachers were paid tax money to read them.[18] Rather they enunciated a more general principle: taken together, the two religion clauses forbade the state either to promote or to inhibit religion. In the words of an earlier decision, they erected a "wall of separation" between church and state.[19]

Few Supreme Court decisions have generated such controversy as those in the school-prayer cases. Efforts to overturn the decisions included proposals to limit the jurisdiction of the Supreme Court and to impeach its then Chief Justice, as well as to amend the Constitution itself. Yet history surely confirms that religion itself as well as the public peace is endangered when governments take sides in sensitive religious matters. Guarding against these dangers is what the Establishment Clause is all about; the last thing we need is for the government to tell us how to pray.

The separation of church and state does not mean, of course, that secular and religious commands may never coincide. That theft and murder are condemned as sins does not prevent their being punished as crimes. Similarly, because a law forbidding Sunday labor served the legitimate secular purpose of providing a uniform day of rest, the Supreme Court refused to find it a forbidden endorsement of the Fourth Commandment.[20] Where no such secular purpose can be found, however, as in the posting of the Ten Commandments themselves in public schools, there is an establishment of religion.[21]

The most challenging problems in interpreting the Establishment Clause have arisen in connection with public support for private schools. Many private schools are religious, and many pupils attend them precisely because they provide spiritual as well as worldly education. To what extent, if at all, may the state support them?

One might expect the answer to be that the state may support their secular but not their religious instruction. It is true that every dollar received for teaching mathematics frees up a dollar for teaching religion. Yet the religious is thus aided only to the extent its proponents elect to promote the secular; the religious institution is no better off than if it gave no worldly lessons at all. Indeed the *exclusion* of religious schools from an otherwise general subsidy of private education would pose serious problems under the Free Exercise Clause: No one should be denied public support for secular education because he also teaches religion at his own expense.

For these reasons the Supreme Court held that the states need not exclude hospitals run by religious bodies from a general hospital subsidy[22] nor parochial-school pupils from a state program providing secular books.[23] Similarly, colleges with religious affiliations were permitted to participate in general programs subsidizing teachers' salaries and new buildings—so long as no public money was used for religious purposes.[24]

The Court was more squeamish, however, with respect to primary schools. In that context, said the Court in *Lemon v. Kurtzman* in 1971, secular and religious education were so tightly interwoven that it would be practically impossible to support one without supporting the other. Any effort to separate the two, the Court continued, would so entangle the state in the administration of the religious body as to impair its independence; and such an "entanglement" would offend a central purpose of the Establishment Clause.[25]

The upshot seemed to be that parochial schools must do without public support so long as they insisted on commingling religious and secular education. In *Mueller v. Allen*, however, a majority of the Justices found a way out: tax deductions for all costs of public or private education.[26]

These deductions had both legitimate purposes and legitimate effects: secular education and the promotion of educational variety and independence. Furthermore, because it was unnecessary to separate the costs of religious and of secular instruction, there was no risk of entanglement. The difficulty was that in the absence of such a separation the tax benefits served also to support religious activities—and not simply, as in the Sunday law case, as the inevitable byproduct of a wholly secular measure. The contrast was startling: *Lemon* had forbidden the state to support even secular instruction; *Mueller* allowed it to support religious instruction too.

The Court attempted in *Mueller* to distinguish earlier decisions invalidating other programs aiding parochial schools. First, the benefits in *Mueller* were given to the pupils' parents; religion was aided only by the private decision to send children to parochial schools.

Even direct subsidies, however, are likely to depend upon the number of pupils and thus on the same private choices. The Justices conceded that the practical effect of the deductions was "comparable" to that of a subsidy; and it had long been established that the effect of a measure posing no problems of purpose or entanglement was determinative.[27]

If the result in *Mueller* can be justified, it is on a second ground also emphasized in the opinion. The state allowed deductions for *all* pupils, not only for those in parochial schools; and it allowed deductions for charitable and medical expenditures as well. The implication is clear: If the state affords benefits to the public generally, it need not discriminate against religious activities.

If the church burns, for example, the state may put out the fire—and not only because of the risk that it may spread to secular buildings. Otherwise the church owner would be disadvantaged because religion was practiced there; and that would offend the Free Exercise Clause. If the state puts out other fires, it not only may but must put out this one, although the church serves only religious purposes.

Similarly, in *Everson v. Board of Education* the Court held that a state could pay for transporting pupils to parochial schools, though the effect was to promote spiritual as well as worldly education.[28] More recently, the Court permitted a student to finance his preparation for the ministry with funds from a general state program of aid to the blind.[29] In the same category is the otherwise inexplicable decision in *Walz v. Tax Commission*, allowing a state to exempt religious bodies from property taxes; as the Justices remarked, other nonprofit organizations enjoyed similar exemptions.[30]

These last decisions and others like them[31] clear the way for a return to the attractive position that the First Amendment requires discrimination neither in favor of religion as in *Yoder* nor against it as in *Lemon*, but rather official neutrality.[32] Like race, religion should play no role in public policy.

9   Conclusion

THE ADOPTION OF THE Constitution was an astonishing achievement. By establishing separate and democratically elected legislative and executive branches and empowering independent judges
to enforce a catalog of fundamental rights, our eighteenth-century
forebears constructed an exemplary framework for government by
and for the people.

Over its first two hundred years, moreover, the Constitution has
worn remarkably well. The wise decision to limit the document to
fundamental principles contributed to this staying power by nour-
ishing the healthy conviction that its provisions should not be disturbed without compelling reasons. Equally decisive, however, is the
fact that the Constitution was built upon such sound principles that
even after two centuries, with only two major alterations since the virtually contemporaneous addition of the Bill of Rights, it continues to
serve the needs of a just and well-ordered society.

Those changes are the significant weakening of constitutional federalism[1] and the guarantee of racial equality.[2] The latter was accom-
plished by the prescribed method of constitutional amendment, the
former in large part by interpretation.

In permitting Congress to assume powers the Constitution appeared to reserve to the states, the Supreme Court demonstrated the
limitations of judicial review as an instrument for enforcing constitutional restrictions. In other times of crisis too the Court has proved
unable to prevent other branches from exceeding their authority.
When Congress effectively reduced the Southern states to colonies
after the Civil War, the judges lacked the courage to intervene.[3] The
Court was unable or unwilling to protect freedom of expression from

the hysteria of the First World War or of the 1950s,[4] and it did little to prevent either executive assumption of congressional war powers or the creation of a "headless fourth branch" of independent agencies.[5] Finally, even favorable decisions of the Supreme Court failed to effectuate the voting rights of African Americans until other branches of the federal government finally added their weight to the scale.[6]

On other occasions, moreover, the judges have so exercised their awesome power of judicial review as to deprive the people of what seemed the legitimate fruits of the democratic process. On the threshold of the Civil War the Court impeded a political solution by a cramped interpretation of Congress's power to legislate for the territories.[7] Before and during the Great Depression the Court repeatedly throttled efforts to ameliorate social ills with the due-process weapon it had essentially fashioned out of whole cloth.[8] A generation later, in the eyes of many, it repeated the error with its controversial abortion decisions.[9]

Judicial review has thus paradoxically proved weak and dangerous at the same time. On the one hand, the judges have not always had the strength to enforce the Constitution in opposition to the spirit of the times. On the other, they have occasionally substituted their own principles for those laid down in the Constitution by the sovereign people.

Nevertheless I believe that on the whole judicial review has served us well. Decisions unjustifiably restricting the democratic process have been relatively rare. Most of them were based on the largely abandoned doctrine of substantive due process, and it would not be surprising if the modern vestige of that doctrine were also to disappear in the next few years. Wrong decisions as well as right ones have a way of yielding ultimately to the spirit of the times; the courts are truly, as Alexander Hamilton wrote, "the least dangerous branch."[10]

The inability of the judges to prevent *every* violation of the Constitution is no reason to abolish judicial review; pretty clearly there

would have been even more violations without it. Despite their insti-
tutional weakness, the courts have often succeeded in enforcing constitutional limitations against other organs of government. After the
Civil War the Supreme Court protected citizens from military trials
and retroactive punishments.[11] A long series of decisions over the past
half century has ensured the fairness of criminal trials.[12] Since the
1950s the Justices have done yeoman service to make racial equality,
the separation of church and state, and the democratic process a reality.[13] Above all, time and time again the Court has protected freedom
of expression from ham-handed governmental invasion.[14] This alone
is enough to justify judicial review; the harm done by occasionally
overzealous judges seems trivial in comparison.

The judges are like referees in a sporting match. We accept their
decisions because someone must have the last word. This means that
judges have effective power, though not authority, to alter the Constitution.

They should resist this temptation with every ounce of their
strength. The Constitution is a law that binds the judges too; even in
football we expect the referee to follow the rules.[15] When the Constitution needs changing, as George Washington warned us in his
Farewell Address, it should be amended according to the procedures
prescribed in article V, not ignored. For usurpation, as Washington
observed, "is the customary weapon by which free governments are
destroyed." If we take liberties with the Constitution in order to im-
prove it, we weaken its power to deliver us from evil.

APPENDIX A

Chronology

1776   Continental Congress adopts Declaration of Independence.

1778   Continental Congress proposes Articles of Confederation.

1781   Articles of Confederation take effect on ratification by thirteenth state.

1783   Treaty of Paris confirms independence of United States.

1787   Philadelphia Convention proposes new Constitution.

1788   Constitution takes effect on ratification by ninth state.

1789   George Washington takes office as first President.
        First Congress meets, establishes federal courts.
        Congress proposes Bill of Rights.
        John Jay named first Chief Justice.

1791   Bill of Rights takes effect on state ratification.

1793   Chisholm v. Georgia allows suit against state.

1795   Senate refuses to confirm John Rutledge as Chief Justice.
        Eleventh Amendment overrules Chisholm, limits suits against states.

1796   Oliver Ellsworth appointed Chief Justice.
        Ware v. Hylton establishes judicial review of state laws.

1801   President Adams appoints John Marshall Chief Justice.
        Federalists lose executive and legislative power following election of Thomas Jefferson.

1803   Marbury v. Madison establishes judicial review of federal statutes and executive acts.

1804   Twelfth Amendment requires electors to vote separately for President and Vice-President.

1805   Unsuccessful impeachment of Justice Samuel Chase.

1810   Fletcher v. Peck holds Contract Clause forbids state to re-
        voke land grant.
1811   Joseph Story appointed Associate Justice.
1816   Martin v. Hunter's Lessee establishes Supreme Court review
        of state-court decisions.
1819   Dartmouth College case holds Contract Clause protects
        corporate charters.
        McCulloch v. Maryland upholds National Bank and its im-
        munity from state tax.
1824   Gibbons v. Ogden upholds federal steamboat license.
1833   Barron v. Baltimore holds Bill of Rights inapplicable to states.
1835   Death of John Marshall.
1836   Roger B. Taney appointed Chief Justice.
1851   Cooley decision confirms that Commerce Clause limits
        state authority.
1857   Dred Scott decision holds blacks not citizens and Congress
        without power to forbid slavery in territories.
1861   Outbreak of Civil War upon attempted secession of eleven
        Southern states.
1864   Prize Cases uphold President Lincoln's authority to blockade
        Confederate ports.
        Death of Chief Justice Taney.
1865   Civil War ends.
        Salmon P. Chase appointed Chief Justice.
        President Lincoln assassinated.
        Thirteenth Amendment abolishes slavery.
1866   Civil Rights Act grants blacks citizenship, equal privileges
        and immunities, and equal protection of law.
        Ex parte Milligan invalidates military trials of civilians.
        Cummings and Garland decisions invalidate anti-Confed-
        erate loyalty oaths.

1867   Reconstruction Act institutes military government in conquered South.

1868   Fourteenth Amendment makes persons born in United States citizens, guarantees privileges and immunities, equal protection, and due process of law.

1869   Ex parte McCardle upholds limitation of Supreme Court jurisdiction, declines to determine validity of military courts in South.

Texas v. White confirms unconstitutionality of secession.

1870   Fifteenth Amendment forbids racial discrimination in voting.

Hepburn v. Griswold holds Congress may not make paper money legal tender.

1871   Legal Tender Cases overrule Hepburn, uphold paper tender.

1873   The Slaughterhouse Cases narrowly interpret Fourteenth Amendment.

1874   Morrison R. Waite appointed Chief Justice.

1879   Reynolds v. United States holds First Amendment does not exempt Mormons from polygamy ban.

1883   Civil Rights Cases hold Congress may not ban private race discrimination.

1888   Melville W. Fuller appointed Chief Justice.

1895   E.C. Knight case holds Sherman Act inapplicable to manufacturers.

Pollock v. Farmers' Loan Co. invalidates federal income tax.

1896   Plessy v. Ferguson upholds "separate but equal" trains.

1903   Oliver Wendell Holmes appointed Associate Justice.

1904   McCray v. United States upholds prohibitive federal tax on margarine.

1905   Lochner v. New York invalidates maximum-hour law.

1908   Ex parte Young allows suit to enjoin state officer.

1910   Edward D. White appointed Chief Justice.

1913   Sixteenth Amendment authorizes unapportioned federal income tax.

Seventeenth Amendment provides for popular election of Senators.

1914   Shreveport case upholds federal authority over local rail rates.

1915   Guinn v. United States invalidates grandfather clause for voting.

1916   Louis D. Brandeis appointed Associate Justice.

1919   Schenck v. United States enunciates clear and present danger test for subversive speech.

Eighteenth Amendment prohibits manufacture and sale of liquor.

1920   William H. Taft appointed Chief Justice.

Nineteenth Amendment extends vote to women.

1923   Adkins v. Children's Hospital invalidates minimum-wage law.

1926   Myers v. United States affirms presidential control of postmasters.

1930   Charles Evans Hughes appointed Chief Justice.

1931   Justice Holmes resigns from Supreme Court.

1932   Powell v. Alabama recognizes right to counsel in state criminal case.

Crowell v. Benson approves quasi-judicial administrative agency.

1933   Twentieth Amendment shortens interval between election and inauguration.

Twenty-first Amendment repeals Eighteenth (prohibition).

1935–36 Supreme Court invalidates New Deal measures and New York minimum-wage law, upholds independence of Federal Trade Commission.

1937   President Roosevelt proposes to "pack" Supreme Court.

Supreme Court upholds minimum-wage law, National Labor Relations Act, and Social Security.

Hugo L. Black appointed Associate Justice.

1938   Carolene Products case suggests stricter scrutiny to protect Bill of Rights, political process, and insular minorities.

1939   Felix Frankfurter appointed Associate Justice.

1941   Harlan F. Stone appointed Chief Justice.

1942   Wickard v. Filburn upholds federal regulation of farming.

1943   West Virginia v. Barnette invalidates compulsory flag salute.

1944   Smith v. Allwright invalidates white primary.

Korematsu v. United States upholds exclusion of Japanese-Americans from West Coast.

1946   Fred M. Vinson appointed Chief Justice.

1947   Everson v. Board of Education holds Establishment Clause applicable to states.

Justice Black announces incorporation theory in Adamson dissent.

1948   Shelley v. Kraemer forbids state to enforce racial restrictive covenant.

1951   Dennis v. United States upholds conviction of leading Communists.

Twenty-second Amendment limits President to two terms.

1952   Youngstown decision holds President may not seize steel mills.

1953   Earl Warren appointed Chief Justice.

1954   Brown v. Board of Education outlaws school segregation.

1958   NAACP v. Alabama forbids state to obtain list of NAACP members.

1959   Barenblatt v. United States rejects First Amendment objection to investigation of subversion.

1961   Twenty-third Amendment authorizes District of Columbia to choose presidential electors.

Mapp v. Ohio requires courts to exclude unlawfully obtained evidence.

1962   Baker v. Carr holds courts may determine validity of legislative apportionment.

Engel v. Vitale outlaws state-sponsored school prayers.

1964   Reynolds v. Sims requires equal legislative apportionment.

Twenty-fourth Amendment outlaws poll taxes in federal elections.

1965   Voting Rights Act requires preclearance of state election laws.

1966   South Carolina v. Katzenbach upholds Voting Rights Act.

1967   Twenty-fifth Amendment provides for presidential disability.

1969   Brandenburg v. Ohio sharpens clear and present danger test.

Warren Burger appointed Chief Justice.

1971   Twenty-sixth Amendment extends vote to 18-year-olds.

1973   Roe v. Wade invalidates abortion ban.

1974   President Nixon resigns after House Judiciary Committee recommends impeachment.

1976   Virginia Pharmacy case holds commercial speech protected.

1978   Bakke case strikes down minimum quota for black students.

1980   Fullilove v. Klutznick upholds minimum quota for minority contractors.

1986   William Rehnquist appointed Chief Justice.

1987   Two hundredth anniversary of Philadelphia Convention.

1988   Morrison v. Olson upholds special-prosecutor law.

1989   200th anniversary of new government under the Constitution.

1990   Smith decision holds Free Exercise does not require religious exemptions from generally applicable laws.

1992   Conservative Court surprisingly reaffirms Roe v. Wade.

Congress and executive branch certify adoption of Twenty-

Seventh Amendment postponing alterations in congressional salary.

1995   United States v. Lopez revives limits on congressional authority.

Supreme Court invalidates term limits for members of Congress.

Adarand decision requires strict scrutiny of racial preferences for minorities.

1996   Romer v. Evans invalidates ban on laws protecting homosexuals from discrimination.

Seminole Tribe v. Florida holds Congress cannot authorize suits against states under Commerce Clause.

1997   Clinton v. Jones allows damage suit against President.

Printz v. United States holds Congress may not coopt state officers to enforce federal law.

1998   Clinton v. City of New York invalidates item-veto legislation.

House impeaches President Clinton for perjury and obstruction of justice.

1999   Senate acquits President Clinton after impeachment trial.

Alden v. Maine holds Commerce Clause does not empower Congress to make states suable in their own courts.

APPENDIX B

The Constitution of the United States of America

WE THE PEOPLE OF THE UNITED STATES, in order to form a more perfect union, establish justice, insure domestic tranquility, provide for the common defense, promote the general welfare, and secure the blessings of liberty to ourselves and our posterity, do ordain and establish this Constitution for the United States of America.

ARTICLE I

Section 1. All legislative powers herein granted shall be vested in a Congress of the United States, which shall consist of a Senate and House of Representatives.

Section 2. The House of Representatives shall be composed of members chosen every second year by the people of the several States, and the electors in each State shall have the qualifications requisite for electors of the most numerous branch of the State legislature.

No person shall be a representative who shall not have attained to the age of twenty-five years, and been seven years a citizen of the United States, and who shall not, when elected, be an inhabitant of that State in which he shall be chosen.

Representatives and direct taxes shall be apportioned among the several States which may be included within this Union, according to their respective numbers, which shall be determined by adding to the whole number of free persons, including those bound to service for a term of years, and excluding Indians not taxed, three fifths of all other persons. The actual enumeration shall be made within three years after the first meeting of the Congress of the United States, and within every subsequent term of ten years, in such manner as they shall by law direct. The number of Representatives shall not exceed one for every thirty thousand, but each State shall have at least one Representative; and until such enumeration shall be made, the State of New Hampshire shall be entitled to choose three, Massachusetts eight, Rhode Island and Providence Plantations one, Connecticut five, New York six, New Jersey four, Pennsylvania eight, Delaware one, Maryland six, Virginia ten, North Carolina five, South Carolina five, and Georgia three.

When vacancies happen in the representation from any State, the executive authority thereof shall issue writs of election to fill such vacancies.

The House of Representatives shall choose their Speaker and other officers; and shall have the sole power of impeachment.

Section 3. The Senate of the United States shall be composed of two Senators from each State, chosen by the legislature thereof, for six years; and each Senator shall have one vote.

Immediately after they shall be assembled in consequence of the first election, they shall be divided as equally as may be into three classes. The seats of the Senators of the first class shall be vacated at the expiration of the second year, of the second class at the expiration of the fourth year, and of the third class at the expiration of the sixth year, so that one third may be chosen every second year; and if vacancies happen by resignation, or otherwise, during the recess of the legislature of any State, the executive thereof may make temporary appointments until the next meeting of the legislature, which shall then fill such vacancies.

No person shall be a Senator who shall not have attained to the age of thirty years, and been nine years a citizen of the United States, and who shall not, when elected, be an inhabitant of that State for which he shall be chosen.

The Vice-President of the United States shall be President of the Senate, but shall have no vote, unless they be equally divided.

The Senate shall choose their other officers, and also a President pro tempore, in the absence of the Vice-President, or when he shall exercise the office of President of the United States.

The Senate shall have the sole power to try all impeachments. When sitting for that purpose, they shall be on oath or affirmation. When the President of the United States is tried, the Chief Justice shall preside: And no person shall be convicted without the concurrence of two thirds of the Members present.

Judgment in cases of impeachment shall not extend further than to removal from office, and disqualification to hold and enjoy any office of honor, trust or profit under the United States: but the party convicted shall nevertheless be liable and subject to indictment, trial, judgment and punishment, according to law.

Section 4. The times, places and manner of holding elections for Senators and Representatives shall be prescribed in each State by the legislature thereof; but the Congress may at any time by law make or alter such regulations, except as to the place of choosing Senators.

The Congress shall assemble at least once in every year, and such meeting shall be on the first Monday in December, unless they shall by law appoint a different day.

Section 5. Each House shall be the judge of the elections, returns and qualifications of its own Members, and a majority of each shall constitute a quorum to do business; but a smaller number may adjourn from day to day, and may be authorized to compel the attendance of absent Members, in such manner, and under such penalties as each House may provide.

Each House may determine the rules of its proceedings, punish its Members for disorderly behavior, and, with the concurrence of two thirds, expel a Member.

Each House shall keep a journal of its proceedings, and from time to time publish the same, excepting such parts as may in their judgment require secrecy; and the yeas and nays of the Members of either House on any question shall, at the desire of one fifth of those present, be entered on the journal.

Neither House, during the session of Congress, shall, without the consent of the other, adjourn for more than three days, nor to any other place than that in which the two Houses shall be sitting.

Section 6. The Senators and Representatives shall receive a compensation for their services, to be ascertained by law, and paid out of the Treasury of the United States. They shall in all cases, except treason, felony and breach of the peace, be privileged from arrest during their attendance at the session of their respective Houses, and in going to and returning from the same; and for any speech or debate in either House, they shall not be questioned in any other place.

No Senator or Representative shall, during the time for which he was elected, be appointed to any civil office under the authority of the United States, which shall have been created, or the emoluments whereof shall have been increased during such time; and no person holding any office under the United States, shall be a Member of either House during his continuance in office.

Section 7. All bills for raising revenue shall originate in the House of Representatives; but the Senate may propose or concur with amendments as on other bills.

Every bill which shall have passed the House of Representatives and the Senate, shall, before it become a law, be presented to the President of the United States. If he approve he shall sign it, but if not he shall return it, with his objections, to that House in which it shall have originated, who shall enter the objections at large on their journal, and proceed to reconsider it. If after such reconsideration two thirds of that House shall agree to pass the bill, it shall be sent, together with the objections, to the other House, by which it shall likewise be reconsidered, and if approved by two thirds of that House, it shall become a law. But in all such cases the votes of both Houses shall be determined by yeas and nays, and the names of the persons voting for and against the bill shall be entered on the journal of each House respectively. If any bill shall not be returned by the President within ten days (Sundays excepted) after it shall have been presented to him, the same shall be a law, in like manner as if he had signed it, unless the Congress by their adjournment prevent its return, in which case it shall not be a law.

Every order, resolution, or vote to which the concurrence of the Senate and House of Representatives may be necessary (except on a question of adjournment) shall be presented to the President of the United States; and before the same shall take effect, shall be approved by him, or being disapproved by him, shall be repassed by two thirds of the Senate and House of Representatives, according to the rules and limitations prescribed in the case of a bill.

Section 8. The Congress shall have power to lay and collect taxes, duties, imposts and excises, to pay the debts and provide for the common defense and general welfare of the United States; but all duties, imposts and excises shall be uniform throughout the United States;

To borrow money on the credit of the United States;

To regulate commerce with foreign nations, and among the several States, with the Indian tribes;

To establish a uniform rule of naturalization, and uniform laws on the subject of bankruptcies throughout the United States;

To coin money, regulate the value thereof, and of foreign coin, and fix the standard of weights and measures;

To provide for the punishment of counterfeiting the securities and current coin of the United States;

To establish post offices and post roads;

To promote the progress of science and useful arts, by securing for limited times to authors and inventors the exclusive right to their respective writings and discoveries;

To constitute tribunals inferior to the Supreme Court;

To define and punish piracies and felonies committed on the high seas, and offenses against the law of nations;

To declare war, grant letters of marque and reprisal, and make rules concerning captures on land and water;

To raise and support armies, but no appropriation of money to that use shall be for a longer term than two years;

To provide and maintain a navy;

To make rules for the government and regulation of the land and naval forces;

To provide for calling forth the militia to execute the laws of the Union, suppress insurrections and repel invasions;

To provide for organizing, arming, and disciplining the militia, and for governing such part of them as may be employed in the service of the United States, reserving to the States respectively, the appointment of the officers, and the authority of training the militia according to the discipline prescribed by Congress;

To exercise exclusive legislation in all cases whatsoever, over such District (not exceeding ten miles square) as may, by cession of particular States, and the acceptance of Congress, become the seat of the government of the United States, and to exercise like authority over all places purchased by the consent of the legislature of the State in which the same shall be, for the erection of forts, magazines, arsenals, dockyards, and other needful buildings;—And

To make all laws which shall be necessary and proper for carrying into execution the foregoing powers, and all other powers vested by this Constitution in the government of the United States, or in any department or officer thereof.

Section 9. The migration or importation of such persons as any of the States now existing shall think proper to admit, shall not be prohibited by the Congress prior to the year one thousand eight hundred and eight, but a tax or duty may be imposed on such importation, not exceeding ten dollars for each person.

The privilege of the writ of habeas corpus shall not be suspended, unless when in cases of rebellion or invasion the public safety may require it.

No bill of attainder or ex post facto law shall be passed.

No capitation, or other direct, tax shall be laid, unless in proportion to the census or enumeration herein before directed to be taken.

To tax or duty shall be laid on articles exported from any State.

No preference shall be given by any regulation of commerce or revenue to the ports of one state over those of another; nor shall vessels bound to, or from, one state, be obliged to enter, clear, or pay duties in another.

No money shall be drawn from the Treasury, but in consequence of appropriations made by law: and a regular statement and account of the receipts and expenditures of all public money shall be published from time to time.

No title of nobility shall be granted by the United States: And no person holding any office of profit or trust under them, shall, without the consent of the Congress, accept of any present, emolument, office, or title, of any kind whatever, from any king, prince, or foreign State.

Section 10. No State shall enter into any treaty, alliance, or confederation; grant letters of marque and reprisal; coin money; emit bills of credit; make any thing but gold and silver coin a tender in payment of debts; pass any bill of attainder, ex post facto law, or law impairing the obligation of contracts, or grant any title of nobility.

No State shall, without the consent of the Congress, lay any imposts or duties on imports or exports, except what may be absolutely necessary for executing its inspection laws: and the net produce of all duties and imposts, laid by any State on imports or exports, shall be for the use of the Treasury of the United States; and all such laws shall be subject to the revision and control of the Congress.

No State shall, without the consent of Congress, lay any duty of tonnage, keep troops, or ships of war in time of peace, enter into any agreement or compact with another State or with a foreign power, or engage in war, unless actually invaded, or in such imminent danger as will not admit of delay.

ARTICLE II

Section 1. The executive power shall be vested in a President of the United States of America. He shall hold his office during the term of four years, and, together with the Vice-President, chosen for the same term, be elected, as follows.

Each State shall appoint, in such manner as the legislature thereof may direct, a number of electors equal to the whole number of Senators and Representatives to which the State may be entitled in the Congress: but no Senator or Representative, or person holding an office of trust or profit under the United States, shall be appointed an elector.

The electors shall meet in their respective States, and vote by ballot for two persons, of whom one at least shall not be an inhabitant of the same State with themselves. And they shall make a list of all the persons voted for, and of the number of votes for each; which list they shall sign and certify, and transmit sealed to the seat of the government of the United States, directed to the President of the Senate. The President of the Senate shall, in the presence of the Senate and House of Representatives, open all the certificates, and the votes shall then be counted. The person having the greatest number of votes shall be the President, if such number be a majority of the whole number of electors appointed; and if there be more than one who have such majority, and have an equal number of votes, then the House of Representatives shall immediately choose by ballot one of them for President; and if no person have a majority, then from the five highest on the list the said House shall in like manner choose the President. But in choosing the President, the votes shall be taken by States, the representation from each State having one vote; a quorum for this purpose shall consist of a Member or Members from two thirds of the States, and a majority of all the States shall be necessary to a choice. In every case, after the choice of the President, the person having the greatest number of votes of the electors shall be the Vice-President. But if there should remain two or more who have equal votes, the Senate shall choose from them by ballot the Vice-President.

The Congress may determine the time of choosing the electors, and the day on which they shall give their votes; which day shall be the same throughout the United States.

No person except a natural born citizen, or a citizen of the United States, at the time of the adoption of this Constitution, shall be eligible to the office of President; neither shall any person be eligible to that office who shall not have attained to the age of thirty-five years, and been fourteen years a resident within the United States.

In case of the removal of the President from office, or of his death, resignation, or inability to discharge the powers and duties of the said office, the same shall devolve on the Vice-President, and the Congress may by law provide for the case of removal, death, resignation or inability, both of the President and Vice President, declaring what officer shall then act as President, and such officer shall act accordingly, until the disability be removed, or a President shall be elected.

The President shall, at stated times, receive for his services, a compensation, which shall neither be increased nor diminished during the period for which he shall have been elected, and he shall not receive within that period any other emolument from the United States, or any of them.

Before he enter on the execution of his office, he shall take the following oath or affirmation:—"I do solemnly swear (or affirm) that I will faithfully execute the office of President of the United States, and will to the best of my ability preserve, protect and defend the Constitution of the United States."

Section 2. The President shall be Commander in Chief of the Army and Navy of the United States, and of the militia of the several States, when called into the actual service of the United States; he may require the opinion in writing, of the principal officer in each of the executive departments, upon any subject relating to the duties of their respective offices, and he shall have power to grant reprieves and pardons for offenses against the United States, except in cases of impeachment.

He shall have power, by and with the advice and consent of the Senate, to make treaties, provided two thirds of the Senators present concur; and he shall nominate, and by and with the advice and consent of the Senate, shall appoint ambassadors, other public ministers and consuls, judges of the Supreme Court, and all other officers of the United States, whose appointments are not herein otherwise provided for, and which shall be established by law: but the Congress may by law vest the appointment of such inferior officers, as they think proper, in the President alone, in the courts of law, or in the heads of departments.

The President shall have power to fill up all vacancies that may happen during the recess of the Senate, by granting commissions which shall expire at the end of their next session.

Section 3. He shall from time to time give to the Congress information of the state of the Union, and recommend to their consideration such measures as he shall judge necessary and expedient; he may, on extraordinary occasions, convene both Houses, or either of them, and in case of disagreement between them, with respect to the time of adjournment, he may adjourn them to such time as he shall think proper; he shall receive ambassadors and other public ministers; he shall take care that the laws be faithfully executed, and shall commission all the officers of the United States.

Section 4. The President, Vice-President and all civil officers of the United States shall be removed from office on impeachment for, and conviction of, treason, bribery, or other high crimes and misdemeanors.

Section 1. The judicial power of the United States shall be vested in one Supreme Court, and in such inferior courts as the Congress may from time to time ordain and establish. The judges, both of the supreme and inferior courts, shall hold their offices during good behavior, and shall, at stated times, receive for their services, a compensation, which shall not be diminished during their continuance in office.

Section 2. The judicial power shall extend to all cases, in law and equity, arising under this Constitution, the laws of the United States, and treaties made, or which shall be made, under their authority;—to all cases affecting ambassadors, other public ministers, and consuls;—to all cases of admiralty and maritime jurisdiction;—to controversies to which the United States shall be a party;—to controversies between two or more States;—between a State and citizens of another State;—between citizens of different States;—between citizens of the same State claiming lands under grants of different States, and between a State, or the citizens thereof, and foreign states, citizens or subjects.

In all cases affecting ambassadors, other public ministers, and consuls, and those in which a State shall be party, the Supreme Court shall have original jurisdiction. In all the other cases before mentioned, the Supreme Court shall have appellate jurisdiction, both as to law and fact, with such exceptions, and under such regulations, as the Congress shall make.

The trial of all crimes, except in cases of impeachment, shall be by jury; and such trial shall be held in the State where the said crimes shall have been committed; but when no committed within any State, the trial shall be at such place or places as the Congress may by law have directed.

Section 3. Treason against the United States, shall consist only in levying war against them, or in adhering to their enemies, giving them aid and comfort. No person shall be convicted of treason unless on the testimony of two witnesses to the same overt act, or on confession in open court.

The Congress shall have power to declare the punishment of treason, but no attainder of treason shall work corruption of blood, or forfeiture except during the life of the person attainted.

ARTICLE IV

Section 1. Full faith and credit shall be given in each State to the public acts, records, and judicial proceedings of every other State. And the Congress may be general laws prescribe the manner in which such acts, records and proceedings shall be proved, and the effect thereof.

Section 2. The citizens of each State shall be entitled to all privileges and immunities of citizens in the several States.

A person charged in any State with treason, felony, or other crime, who shall flee from justice, and be found in another State, shall on demand of the executive authority of the State from which he fled, be delivered up to be removed to the State having jurisdiction of the crime.

No person held to service or labor in one State, under the laws thereof, escaping into another, shall, in consequence of any law or regulation therein, be discharged from such service or labor, but shall be delivered up on claim of the party to whom such service or labor may be due.

Section 3. New States may be admitted by the Congress into this Union; but no new State shall be formed or erected within the jurisdiction of any other State; nor any State be formed by the junction of two or more States, or parts of States, without the consent of the legislatures of the States concerned as well as of the Congress.

The Congress shall have power to dispose of and make all needful rules and regulations respecting the territory or other property belonging to the United States; and nothing in this Constitution shall be so construed as to prejudice any claims of the United States, or of any particular State.

Section 4. The United States shall guarantee to every State in this Union a republican form of government, and shall protect each of them against invasion; and on application of the legislature, or of the executive (when the legislature cannot be convened) against domestic violence.

ARTICLE V

The Congress, whenever two thirds of both Houses shall deem it necessary, shall propose amendments to this Constitution, or, on the application of the legislatures of two thirds of the several States, shall call a convention for proposing amendments, which, in either case, shall be valid to all intents and purposes, as part of this Constitution, when ratified by the legislatures of three fourths of the several States, or by conventions in three fourths thereof, as the one or the other mode of ratification may be proposed by the Congress: Provided that no amendment which may be made prior to the year one thousand eight hundred and eight shall in any manner affect the first and fourth clauses in the ninth section of the first Article; and that no State, without its consent, shall be deprived of its equal suffrage in the Senate.

ARTICLE VI

All debts contracted and engagements entered into, before the adoption of this Constitution, shall be as valid against the United States under this Constitution, as under the Confederation.

This Constitution, and the laws of the United States which shall be made in pursuance thereof; and all treaties made, or which shall be made, under the authority of the United States, shall be the supreme law of the land, and the judges in every State shall be bound thereby, any thing in the Constitution or laws of any State to the contrary notwithstanding.

The Senators and Representatives before mentioned, and the members of the several state legislatures, and all executive and judicial officers, both of the United States and of the several States, shall be bound by oath or affirmation, to support this Constitution: but no religious test shall ever be required as a qualification to any office or public trust under the United States.

ARTICLE VII

The ratification of the conventions of nine States shall be sufficient for the establishment of this Constitution between the States so ratifying the same.

AMENDMENT I (1791)

Congress shall make no law respecting an establishment of religion, or prohibiting the free exercise thereof; or abridging the freedom of speech, or of the press; or the right of the people peaceably to assemble, and to petition the government for a redress of grievances.

AMENDMENT II (1791)

A well regulated militia being necessary to the security of a free State, the right of the people to keep and bear arms shall not be infringed.

AMENDMENT III (1791)

No soldier shall, in time of peace, be quartered in any house, without the consent of the owner, nor in time of war, but in a manner to be prescribed by law.

Amendment IV (1791)

The right of the people to be secure in their persons, houses, papers, and effects, against unreasonable searches and seizures, shall not be violated, and no warrants shall issue, but upon probable cause, supported by oath or affirmation, and particularly describing the place to be searched, and the persons or things to be seized.

Amendment V (1791)

No person shall be held to answer for a capital, or otherwise infamous crime, unless on a presentment or indictment of a grand jury, except in cases arising in the land or naval forces, or in the militia, when in actual service in time of war or public danger; nor shall any person be subject for the same offense to be twice put in jeopardy of life or limb; nor shall be compelled in any criminal case to be a witness against himself, nor be deprived of life, liberty, or property, without due process of law; nor shall private property be taken for public use, without just compensation.

Amendment VI (1791)

In all criminal prosecutions, the accused shall enjoy the right to a speedy and public trial, by an impartial jury of the State and district wherein the crime shall have been committed, which district shall have been previously ascertained by law, and to be informed of the nature and cause of the accusation; to be confronted with the witnesses against him; to have compulsory process for obtaining witnesses in his favor, and to have the assistance of counsel for his defense.

Amendment VII (1791)

In suits at common law, where the value in controversy shall exceed twenty dollars, the right of trial by jury shall be preserved, and no fact tried by a jury shall be otherwise reexamined in any court of the United States, than according to the rules of the common law.

AMENDMENT VIII (1791)

Excessive bail shall not be required, nor excessive fines imposed, nor cruel and unusual punishments inflicted.

AMENDMENT IX (1791)

The enumeration in the Constitution, of certain rights, shall not be construed to deny or disparage others retained by the people.

AMENDMENT X (1791)

The powers not delegated to the United States by the Constitution, nor prohibited by it to the States, are reserved to the States respectively, or to the people.

AMENDMENT XI (1798)

The judicial power of the United States shall not be construed to extend to any suit in law or equity, commenced or prosecuted against one of the United States by citizens of another State, or by citizens or subjects of any foreign state.

AMENDMENT XII (1804)

The electors shall meet in their respective States and vote by ballot for President and Vice-President, one of whom, at least, shall not be an inhabitant of the same State with themselves: they shall name in their ballots the person voted for as President, and in distinct ballots the person voted for as Vice-President, and they shall make distinct lists of all persons voted for as President, and of all persons voted for as Vice-President, and of the number of votes for each, which lists they shall sign and certify, and transmit sealed to the seat of the Government of the United States, directed to the President of the Senate;—The President of the Senate shall, in presence of the Senate and House of Representatives, open all the certificates and the votes shall then be counted.—The person having the greatest number of votes for President, shall be the President, if such number be a majority of the whole number of electors appointed; and if no person have such majority, then from the persons having the highest numbers not exceeding three on the list of those voted for as President, the House of Representatives shall choose immediately, by ballot, the President. But choosing the President, the votes shall be taken by States, the representation from each State having one vote; a quorum for this purpose shall consist of a member or members from two thirds of the States, and a majority of all the States shall be necessary to a choice. And if the House of Representatives shall not choose a President whenever the right of choice shall devolve upon them, before the fourth day of March next following, then the Vice-President shall act as President, as in the case of the death or other constitutional disability of the President.

The person having the greatest number of votes as Vice-President shall be the Vice-President, if such number be a majority of the whole number of electors appointed; and if no person have a majority, then from the two highest numbers on the list the Senate shall choose the Vice-President; a quorum for the purpose shall consist of two thirds of the whole number of Senators, and a majority of the whole number shall be necessary to a choice. But no person constitutionally ineligible to the office of President shall be eligible to that of Vice-President of the United States.

Amendment XIII (1865)

Section 1. Neither slavery nor involuntary servitude, except as a punishment for crime whereof the party shall have been duly convicted, shall exist within the United States, or any place subject to their jurisdiction.

Section 2. Congress shall have power to enforce this article by appropriate legislation.

AMENDMENT XIV (1868)

Section 1. All persons born or naturalized in the United States, and subject to the jurisdiction thereof, are citizens of the United States and of the State wherein they reside. No State shall make or enforce any law which shall abridge the privileges or immunities of citizens of the United States; nor shall any State deprive any person of life, liberty, or property, without due process of law; nor deny to any person within its jurisdiction the equal protection of the laws.

Section 2. Representatives shall be apportioned among the several States according to their respective numbers, counting the whole number of persons in each State, excluding Indians not taxed. But when the right to vote at any election for the choice of electors for President and Vice-President of the United States, Representatives in Congress, the executive and judicial officers of a State, or the members of the legislature thereof, is denied to any of the male inhabitants of such State, being twenty-one years of age, and citizens of the United States, or in any way abridged, except for participation in rebellion, or other crime, the basis of representation therein shall be reduced in the proportion which the number of such male citizens shall bear to the whole number of male citizens twenty-one years of age in such State.

Section 3. No person shall be a Senator or Representative in Congress, or elector of President and Vice-President, or hold any office, civil or military, under the United States, or under any State, who, having previously taken an oath, as a member of Congress, or as an officer of the United States, or as a member of any state legislature, or as an executive or judicial officer of any State to support the Constitution of the United States, shall have engaged in insurrection or rebellion against the same, or given aid or comfort to the enemies thereof. But Congress may, by a vote of two thirds of each House, remove such disability.

Section 4. The validity of the public debt of the United States, authorized by law, including debts incurred for payment of pensions and bounties for services in suppressing insurrection or rebellion, shall not be questioned. But neither the United States nor any State shall assume or pay any debt or obligation incurred in aid of insurrection or rebellion against the United States, or any claim for the loss or emancipation of any slave; but all such debts, obligations and claims shall be held illegal and void.

Section 5. The Congress shall have power to enforce, by appropriate legislation, the provisions of this article.

Amendment XV (1870)

Section 1. The right of citizens of the United States to vote shall not be denied or abridged by the United States or by any State on account of race, color, or previous condition of servitude.

Section 2. The Congress shall have power to enforce this article by appropriate legislation.

Amendment XVI (1913)

The Congress shall have power to lay and collect taxes on incomes, from whatever source derived, without apportionment among the several States, and without regard to any census or enumeration.

Amendment XVII (1913)

The Senate of the United States shall be composed of two Senators from each State, elected by the people thereof, for six years; and each Senator shall have one vote. The electors in each State shall have the qualifications requisite for electors of the most numerous branch of the state legislatures.

When vacancies happen in the representation of any State in the Senate, the executive authority of such State shall issue writs of election to fill such vacancies: Provided, that the legislature of any State may empower the executive thereof to make temporary appointments until the people fill the vacancies by election as the legislature may direct.

This amendment shall not be so construed as to affect the election or term of any Senator chosen before it becomes valid as part of the Constitution.

AMENDMENT XVIII (1919)

Section 1. After one year from the ratification of this article the manufacture, sale, or transportation of intoxicating liquors within, the importation thereof into, or the exportation thereof from the United States and all territory subject to the jurisdiction thereof for beverage purposes is hereby prohibited.

Section 2. The Congress and the several States shall have concurrent power to enforce this article by appropriate legislation.

Section 3. This article shall be inoperative unless it shall have been ratified as an amendment to the Constitution by the legislatures of the several States as provided in the Constitution, within seven years from the date of the submission hereof to the States by the Congress.

AMENDMENT XIX (1920)

Section 1. The right of citizens of the United States to vote shall not be denied or abridged by the United States or by any State on account of sex.

Section 2. Congress shall have power to enforce this article by appropriate legislation.

AMENDMENT XX (1933)

Section 1. The terms of the President and Vice-President shall end at noon on the 20th day of January, and the terms of Senators and Representatives at noon on the 3d day of January, of the years in which such terms would have ended if this article had not been ratified; and the terms of their successors shall then begin.

Section 2. The Congress shall assemble at least once in every year, and such meeting shall begin at noon on the 3d day of January, unless they shall by law appoint a different day.

Section 3. If, at the time fixed for the beginning of the term of the President, the President elect shall have died, the Vice-President shall become President. If a President shall not have been chosen before the time fixed for the beginning of his term, or if the President elect shall have failed to qualify, then the Vice-President elect shall act as President until a President shall have qualified; and the Congress may by law provide for the case wherein neither a President elect nor a Vice-President elect shall have qualified, declaring who shall then act as President, or the manner in which one who is to act shall be selected, and such person shall act accordingly until a President or Vice-President shall have qualified.

Section 4. The Congress may by law provide for the case of the death of any of the persons from whom the House of Representatives may choose a President whenever the right of choice shall have devolved upon them, and for the case of the death of any of the persons from whom the Senate may choose a Vice-President whenever the right of choice shall have devolved upon them.

Section 5. Sections 1 and 2 shall take effect on the 15th day of October following the ratification of this article.

Section 6. This article shall be inoperative unless it shall have been ratified as an amendment to the Constitution by the legislatures of three fourths of the several States within seven years from the date of its submission.

Amendment XXI (1933)

Section 1. The eighteenth article of amendment to the Constitution of the United States is hereby repealed.

Section 2. The transportation or importation into any State, Territory, or possession of the United States for delivery or use therein of intoxicating liquors, in violation of the laws thereof, is hereby prohibited.

Section 3. This article shall be inoperative unless it shall have been ratified as an amendment to the Constitution by conventions in the several States, as provided in the Constitution, within seven years from the date of the submission hereof to the States by the Congress.

AMENDMENT XXII (1951)

Section 1. No person shall be elected to the office of the President more than twice, and no person who has held the office of President, or acted as President, for more than two years of a term to which some other person was elected President shall be elected to the office of the President more than once. But this Article shall not apply to any person holding the office of President when this Article was proposed by the Congress, and shall not prevent any person who may be holding the office of President, or acting as President, during the term within which this Article becomes operative from holding the office of President or acting as President during the remainder of such term.

Section 2. This article shall be inoperative unless it shall have been ratified as an amendment to the Constitution by the legislatures of three fourths of the several States within seven years from the date of its submission to the States by the Congress.

AMENDMENT XXIII (1961)

Section 1. The District constituting the seat of Government of the United States shall appoint in such manner as the Congress may direct:

A number of electors of President and Vice-President equal to the whole number of Senators and Representatives in Congress to which the District would be entitled if it were a State, but in no event more than the least populous State; they shall be in addition to those appointed by the States, but they shall be considered, for the purposes of the election of President and Vice-President, to be electors appointed by a State: and they shall meet in the District and perform such duties as provided by the twelfth article of amendment.

Section 2. The Congress shall have power to enforce this article by appropriate legislation.

AMENDMENT XXIV (1964)

Section 1. The right of citizens of the United States to vote in any primary or other election for President or Vice-President, for electors for President or Vice-President, or for Senator or Representative in Congress, shall not be denied or abridged by the United States or any State by reason of failure to pay any poll tax or other tax.

Section 2. The Congress shall have power to enforce this article by appropriate legislation.

AMENDMENT XXV (1967)

Section 1. In case of the removal of the President from office or of his death or resignation, the Vice-President shall become President.

Section 2. Whenever there is a vacancy in the office of the Vice-President, the President shall nominate a Vice-President who shall take office upon confirmation by a majority vote of both Houses of Congress.

Section 3. Whenever the President transmits to the President pro tempore of the Senate and the Speaker of the House of Representatives his written declaration that he is unable to discharge the powers and duties of his office, and until he transmits to them a written declaration to the contrary, such powers and duties shall be discharged by the Vice-President as Acting President.

Section 4. Whenever the Vice-President and a majority of either the principal officers of the executive departments or of such other body as Congress may be law provide, transmit to the President pro tempore of the Senate and the Speaker of the House of Representatives their written declaration that the President is unable to discharge the powers and duties of his office, the Vice-President shall immediately assume the powers and duties of the office as Acting President.

Thereafter, when the President transmits to the President pro tempore of the Senate and the Speaker of the House of Representatives his written declaration that no inability exists, he shall resume the powers and duties of his office unless the Vice-President and a majority of either the principal officers of the executive department or of such other body as Congress may by law provide, transmit within four days to the President pro tempore of the Senate and the Speaker of the House of Representatives their written declaration that the President is unable to discharge the powers and duties of his office. Thereupon Congress shall decide the issue, assembling within forty-eight hours for that purpose if not in session. If the Congress, within twenty-one days after receipt of the latter written declaration, or, if Congress is not in session, within twenty-one days after Congress is required to assemble, determines by two-thirds vote of both Houses that the President is unable to discharge the powers and duties of his office, the Vice-President shall continue to discharge the same as Acting President; otherwise, the President shall resume the powers and duties of his office.

AMENDMENT XXVI (1971)

Section 1. The right of citizens of the United States, who are eighteen years of age or older, to vote shall not be denied or abridged by the United States or by any State on account of age.

Section 2. The Congress shall have power to enforce this article by appropriate legislation.

AMENDMENT XXVII (1992)[1]

No law varying the compensation for the services of the Senators and Representatives shall take effect until an election of Representatives has intervened.

NOTES

1. See McCulloch v. Maryland, 17 U.S. 316 (1819).
2. Prigg v. Pennsylvania, 41 U.S. 539, 610–11 (1842).

CHAPTER ONE

1. 1 Stat. 4 (1778).
2. See 2 Records of the Federal Convention 469 (M. Farrand ed. 1966). James Madison also argued that breaches of the articles by some states had absolved the others of their duty to obey them. See 1 id. at 314.
3. See n. 26.
4. See art. I, § 2 (inclusion of "free persons" and three-fifths of "all other persons" in the base for apportioning representatives and direct taxes among the states); art. I, § 9 (twenty-year suspension of congressional authority to ban "migration or importation of such persons" as the states "may think proper to admit"); art. IV, § 2 (requiring states to return fugitives "held to service or labor" in other states); art. V (prohibiting amendment of the slave-trade provision during its limited existence).
5. "No State, without its consent, shall be deprived of its equal suffrage in the Senate."
6. A Representative must be 25 years old, a Senator 30; a Representative must have been a citizen for seven years, a Senator for nine; both must be inhabitants of the state they represent at the time of election. Art. I, §§ 2, 3.
7. U.S. Term Limits, Inc. v. Thornton, 514 U.S. 779 (1995). See also Powell v. McCormack, 395 U.S. 486 (1969).
8. See Pollock v. Farmers' Loan & Trust Co., 157 U.S. 429, modified on rehearing, 158 U.S. 601 (1895).
9. This happened in 1824, when the House chose John Quincy Adams over Andrew Jackson, who had received a greater number of electoral votes.
10. "[I]mpeachment" is the accusation of an officer by the House, not his removal by the Senate. See Art. I, § 2: "The House of Representatives . . . shall have the sole power of impeachment."
11. For discussion of *presidential* power to remove executive officers see chap. 4.

12. United States v. Nixon, 418 U.S. 683 (1974).

13. Nixon v. Fitzgerald, 457 U.S. 731 (1982).

14. 520 U.S. 681 (1997).

15. Jefferson to George Hay, June 17, 1807, in 10 Jefferson Writings (Ford ed.) at 400–401.

16. United States v. Burr, 25 F. Cas. 30, 34 (C.C.D. Va. 1807). See Currie, The President's Evidence, 1 Green Bag 2d 131, 134 (1998).

17. This was essentially the position taken by Justice Breyer in his sensitive concurring opinion in *Clinton*.

18. See United States v. Belmont, 301 U.S. 324 (1937) (authority to recognize foreign governments and conclude ancillary executive agreements).

19. See United States v. Curtiss-Wright Export Corp., 299 U.S. 304 (1936).

20. By treating a bill as a unit ("[i]f he approve he shall sign it, but if not he shall return it"), article I makes clear that the veto is an all-or-nothing proposition; the President may not approve part of a bill and veto the rest. See 33 Writings of George Washington 96 (J. Fitzpatrick ed., 1940) (recognizing that the President must "approve all the parts of a Bill, or reject it in toto"); Clinton v. City of New York, 524 U.S. 417 (1998) (striking down an effort to circumvent this requirement by authorizing the President to "cancel" individual items in bills authorizing expenditures or conferring tax benefits).

21. See The Federalist, nos. 78–79 (Alexander Hamilton).

22. See In re Hennen, 38 U.S. 230, 257–59 (1839).

23. Morrison v. Olson, 487 U.S. 654 (1988).

24. In most instances the Supreme Court has discretion whether or not to accept cases that fall within its appellate jurisdiction; 28 U.S.C. §§ 1254, 1257. This discretion, which has been expanded over the years, is necessary to prevent the Court from being swamped by the sheer volume of litigation.

25. See National Prohibition Cases, 253 U.S. 350 (1920); Leser v. Garnett, 258 U.S. 130 (1922). Before 1808 the provisions of article I dealing with direct taxes and the importation of slaves were also protected against amendment.

26. The so-called Twenty-seventh Amendment, which postpones increases in congressional salaries until after the next election, was ratified by a few states in the eighteenth century, by one in the nineteenth, and by a number of others in the twentieth. It seems obvious that the broad national consensus contemplated by article V was never achieved, but Congress and the executive both proclaimed the amendment's adoption, and the Supreme Court has said it is not for the courts to determine whether an amendment proposal has expired. Coleman v. Miller, 307 U.S. 433 (1939).

27. One of the remaining proposals was ultimately proclaimed as the "Twenty-seventh Amendment," discussed in the preceding footnote. The other, which would have altered the formula for allocating Representatives among the states, was never [yet?] ratified.

28. See Parsons v. Bedford, 28 U.S. 433 (1830).

29. Cummings v. Missouri, 71 U.S. 277 (1867); Ex parte Garland, 71 U.S. 333 (1867).

30. See Fletcher v. Peck, 10 U.S. 87 (land grant); Trustees of Dartmouth College v. Woodward, 17 U.S. 518 (1819) (corporate charter); Home Building & Loan Association v. Blaisdell, 290 U.S. 398 (1934) (upholding a mortgage moratorium law similar to measures that had prompted adoption of the clause). The Contract Clause protects only contracts entered into before the law in question was passed; like the Ex Post Facto Clauses, it is understood to reflect the unfairness of retroactive legislation. See Ogden v. Saunders, 25 U.S. 213 (1827).

31. Barron v. Baltimore, 32 U.S. 243 (1833).

32. 60 U.S. 393 (1857).

33. The only exception is for persons born in the United States but not "subject to their jurisdiction," such as the children of foreign diplomats. Federal law also gives American citizenship to children born to American citizens abroad.

Chapter Two

1. 5 U.S. 137 (1803).

2. J. Thayer, John Marshall 78 (P. Kurland ed. 1967). Several European countries have since adopted judicial review. See, for example, Basic Law for the Federal Republic of Germany, art. 93 I, 100 I.

3. This interpretation would not leave the jurisdictional provision of article III without practical effect, for there are distinct and more compelling arguments for judicial review of other governmental actions, such as those of the states. The text of the Supremacy Clause, for example, shows clearly that the judges were to give the Constitution precedence over conflicting state law: "This Constitution . . . shall be the supreme law of the land; and the judges in every state shall be bound thereby, *any thing in the constitution or laws of any state to the contrary notwithstanding.*" Judicial review of *state* laws was confirmed on the basis of this provision in 1796. Ware v. Hylton, 3 U.S. 199.

4. 1 Convention Records, cited in n. 2 of the Introduction, at 97. See also id. at 109; 2 id. at 73, 76, 78 (remarks of Elbridge Gerry, James Wilson, Luther Martin, and George Mason); The Federalist, no. 78 (Alexander

Hamilton); Corwin, Marbury v. Madison and the Doctrine of Judicial Review, 12 Mich. L. Rev. 538, 543 (1914): "That the members of the Convention of 1787 thought the Constitution secured to courts in the United States the right to pass on the validity of acts of Congress under it cannot be reasonably doubted."

5. 28 U.S.C. § 1331. In suits against *state* officers, Congress has authorized the courts in general terms to take action necessary to remedy violations of constitutional rights. 42 U.S.C. § 1983. In suits against *federal* officers Congress has expressly provided for a declaration of the complaining party's rights as well as for the writs of mandamus to compel action required by law (as in *Marbury* itself) and habeas corpus to remedy unlawful imprisonment. 28 U.S.C. §§ 2201, 1361, 2241. Habeas corpus is guaranteed by the Constitution itself except in emergencies resulting from "rebellion or invasion" (art. I, § 9). Other remedies such as damages and injunctions forbidding unlawful conduct, the Court has held, may also be granted. See Bivens v. Six Unknown Agents, 403 U.S. 388 (1971).

6. Massachusetts v. Mellon, 262 U.S. 447 (1923).

7. Flast v. Cohen, 392 U.S. 83 (1968). See chap. 8.

8. Chisholm v. Georgia, 2 U.S. 419 (1793).

9. 3 J. Elliot, The Debates in the Several State Conventions on the Adoption of the Federal Constitution 533 (2d ed. 1854). See also id. at 555 (John Marshall); The Federalist, no. 81 (Alexander Hamilton); Hans v. Louisiana, 134 U.S. 1 (1890).

10. See, e.g., 5 U.S.C. § 702 (suits for nonmonetary relief against federal officers); 28 U.S.C. § 1346 (a), (b) (certain contract and tort actions).

11. See, e.g., Petty v. Tennessee-Missouri Bridge Commission, 359 U.S. 275 (1959) (stretching the language of an interstate compact to find a waiver of state immunity).

12. Fitzpatrick v. Bitzer, 427 U.S. 445 (1976) (Fourteenth Amendment). Contrast Seminole Tribe v. Florida, 517 U.S. 44 (1996) (a 5-4 decision denying Congress's authority to abrogate a state's immunity by legislation under the Commerce Clause). In 1999, appropriately relying on recent decisions recognizing other implicit intergovernmental immunities (see chap. 3), the Court added that the Commerce Clause did not permit Congress to make states suable in their own courts either. Alden v. Maine, 119 S.Ct. 2240.

13. Ex parte Young, 209 U.S. 123 (1908).

14. Edelman v. Jordan, 415 U.S. 651 (1974). See Currie, Sovereign Immunity and Suits Against Government Officers, 1984 Supreme Court Review 149.

15. Pacific States Tel. & Tel. Co. v. Oregon, 223 U.S. 118 (1912); Cole-

man v. Miller, 307 U.S. 433 (1939). The Court has, however, resolved other issues relating to the ratification of constitutional amendments. See, for example, Hollingsworth v. Virginia, 3 U.S. 378 (1798) (a proposed amendment need not be submitted to the President for possible veto); Dillon v. Gloss, 256 U.S. 368 (1921) (Congress may limit the time for state ratification).

16. See Henkin, Is There a "Political Question" Doctrine?, 85 Yale L.J. 597 (1976).

17. This was the principal reason why the Court recently refused to decide whether article I, § 3 required the Senate itself to hear testimony in an impeachment trial rather than referring the matter to a committee. Nixon v. United States, 506 U.S. 224 (1993). See also The Federalist, no. 65 (Alexander Hamilton), explaining why the courts were thought incapable of exercising this analytically judicial function.

18. The asserted lack of manageable standards was an additional ground for the decision in Nixon v. United States, cited in the preceding note.

19. Baker v. Carr, 369 U.S. 186 (1962) (dissenting opinion).

20. See Baker v. Carr, cited in n. 19; Reynolds v. Sims, 377 U.S. 533 (1964) (holding legislative districts must be substantially equal in population).

21. See, for example, Baker v. Carr, cited in n. 19; Powell v. McCormack, 395 U.S. 486 (1969) (reviewing the action of the House of Representatives in excluding one of its members on grounds not listed in article I, despite the constitutional provision making each chamber of Congress "judge of the elections, returns and qualifications of its members" (art. I, § 5)).

22. Ex parte McCardle, 74 U.S. 506 (1869); Sheldon v. Sill, 49 U.S. 441 (1850).

23. United States v. Klein, 80 U.S. 128 (1872); Yakus v. United States, 327 U.S. 414, 468 (1944) (Rutledge, J., dissenting).

24. See Hart, The Power of Congress to Limit the Jurisdiction of Federal Courts: An Exercise in Dialectic, 66 Harv. L. Rev. 1362, 1365 (1953) (arguing that Congress is not empowered to "destroy the essential role of the Supreme Court in the constitutional plan").

25. See 1 C. Warren, The Supreme Court in United States History 269–315 (rev. ed. 1926); R. Jackson, The Struggle for Judicial Supremacy (1941); S. Rep. no. 711, 75th Cong., 1st Sess. (1937).

26. "A switch in time," as wags noted, "saves nine." See also chap. 3.

CHAPTER THREE

1. The Federalist, no. 45. Similar assurances pervaded the debates in both the national and state conventions.

2. 17 U.S. 316 (1819).

3. See Hepburn v. Griswold, 75 U.S. 603 (1870); Legal Tender Cases, 79 U.S. 457 (1871).

4. See 1 The Works of Alexander Hamilton, 138–41 (1810).

5. The Federalist, no. 45.

6. 22 U.S. 1 .

7. United States v. Coombs, 37 U.S. 72 (1838).

8. Southern Railway v. United States, 222 U.S. 20 (1911).

9. Houston, E. & W. Texas Ry. v. United States (Shreveport Rate Case), 234 U.S. 342 (1914).

10. Wickard v. Filburn, 317 U.S. 111 (1942). See also Katzenbach v. McClung, 379 U.S. 294 (1964), upholding congressional authority to outlaw racial discrimination in a restaurant not even shown to serve interstate travelers, on the ground that restaurants that refused to serve blacks purchased less food from other states.

11. Hamilton v. Kentucky Distilleries Co., 251 U.S. 146 (1919).

12. McCray v. United States, 195 U.S. 27 (1904).

13. South Dakota v. Dole, 483 U.S. 203 (1987). See also Missouri v. Holland, 252 U.S. 416 (1920), holding the President's treaty-making power not limited to the subjects with respect to which Congress may legislate.

14. See, for example, United States v. E.C. Knight Co., 156 U.S. 1 (1895) (construing the antitrust provisions of the Sherman Act not to apply to manufacturing, in order to avoid holding it unconstitutional); Hammer v. Dagenhart, 247 U.S. 251 (1918), and the Child Labor Tax Case, 259 U.S. 20 (1922) (striking down congressional efforts to regulate child labor under the guise of the commerce and tax powers, respectively); A. L. A. Schechter Poultry Co. v. United States, 295 U.S. 495 (1935) (regulation of local butcher's prices, wages, and product quality).

15. See Articles of Confederation, art. 8; The Federalist, nos. 41, 45 (Madison).

16. 514 U.S. 549.

17. *Retroactive* state insolvency laws, however, were held to impair the obligation of contracts in violation of art. I, § 10; and Congress has power to displace even prospective laws in this field by enacting exclusive federal bankruptcy provisions. See Sturges v. Crowninshield, 17 U.S. 122 (1819).

18. This was the view of Chief Justice Roger Taney, Marshall's successor, but he did not speak for a majority of the Justices. See, e.g., License Cases, 46 U.S. 504 (1847).

19. See The Federalist, no. 22 (Hamilton).

20. See, e.g., Gibbons v. Ogden, 22 U.S. 1 (1924); Cooley v. Board of Wardens, 53 U.S. 299 (1852).

21. See, e.g., Gibbons v. Ogden, cited in n. 20 (referring, among other things, to quarantine regulations) and Cooley v. Board of Wardens, also cited in n. 20 (upholding a state law requiring employment of local pilots); Sherlock v. Alling, 93 U.S. 99 (1876) (upholding application of a state law authorizing damages for wrongful death).

22. Southern Pacific Co. v. Arizona, 325 U.S. 761 (1945).

23. Welton v. Missouri, 91 U.S. 275 (1876). See also Philadelphia v. New Jersey, 437 U.S. 617 (1978) (state may not forbid disposal of out-of-state wastes).

24. See Case of the State Freight Tax, 82 U.S. 232 (1873); Western Live Stock v. Bureau of Revenue, 303 U.S. 250 (1938).

25. Compare Bradley v. Public Utilities Commission, 289 U.S. 92 (1933), with Buck v. Kuykendall, 267 U.S. 307 (1925).

26. Compare South Carolina State Highway Dept. v. Barnwell Bros., 303 U.S. 177 (1938), with Southern Pacific Co. v. Arizona, cited in n. 22 above.

27. See, e.g., Johnson v. Maryland, 254 U.S. 51 (1920) (state may not require license to drive postal truck).

28. Panhandle Oil Co. v. Mississippi ex rel. Knox, 277 U.S. 218, 233 (1928) (Holmes, J., dissenting).

29. Bank v. Supervisors, 74 U.S. 26 (1869).

30. See, e.g., Collector v. Day, 78 U.S. 113 (1871).

31. Helvering v. Gerhardt, 304 U.S. 405 (1938); Graves v. New York ex rel. O'Keefe, 306 U.S. 466 (1939).

32. New York v. United States, 326 U.S. 572 (1946).

33. Garcia v. San Antonio Metropolitan Transit Authority, 469 U.S. 528 (1985).

34. First Agricultural National Bank v. State Tax Commission, 392 U.S. 339 (1968) (Thurgood Marshall, J., dissenting).

35. New York v. United States, 505 U.S. 144 (1992); Printz v. United States, 521 U.S. 898 (1997).

CHAPTER FOUR

1. 343 U.S. 579 (1952).

2. The remedy was a court order enjoining the strike. President Truman did not seek to obtain such an injunction.

3. See Ex parte Milligan, 71 U.S. 2 (1866).

4. "The Congress shall have power . . . to make all laws which shall be necessary and proper for carrying into execution the foregoing powers, *and all other powers vested by this Constitution in the Government of the United States, or in any department or officer thereof.*" Art. I, § 8.

5. See The Federalist, nos. 24, 26, 28, 47.

6. See also chap. 5.

7. Art. I, § 1. The same is true of the judicial power, which is defined to extend only to the types of cases and controversies enumerated in article III.

8. See, e.g., McCulloch v. Maryland, cited in chap. 3; Stuart v. Laird, 5 U.S. 299 (1803).

9. 135 U.S. 1 (1890).

10. 158 U.S. 564 (1895).

11. Similarly, it is Congress and not the President that is empowered to engage private armed forces to do battle by issuing "letters of marque and reprisal." See Lobel, Covert War and Congressional Authority: Hidden War and Forgotten Power, 139 U. Pa. L. Rev. 1035 (1986).

12. See 2 Convention Records, cited in the Introduction, at 318.

13. See the Prize Cases, 67 U.S. 635 (1863).

14. The earlier Gulf War in defense of Kuwait was approved in advance by Congress, as the Constitution envisions.

15. See, e.g., Mora v. MacNamara, 389 U.S. 934 (1967).

16. 87 Stat. 555 (1973).

17. Cf. City of Boerne v. Flores, 521 U.S. 507 (1997), noted in chap. 8.

18. These purposes were all clearly expressed in the Constitutional Convention and in the Federalist Papers. See Currie, The Distribution of Powers After *Bowsher*, 1986 Supreme Court Review 19.

19. See 15 U.S.C. § 45. The courts, as will appear below, have only limited authority to review Commission decisions.

20. The Due Process Clause of the Fifth Amendment, moreover, requires that alleged offenders be afforded a fair trial. One of the basic requisites of a fair trial is an unbiased tribunal, and it is difficult to see how the Commission can be impartial in passing upon the sufficiency of its own proof. See chap. 5.

21. See A. L. A. Schechter Poultry Co. v. United States, 295 U.S. 495 (1935). This conclusion was not necessary to the decision, since the Commission's authority was not in issue in the case.

22. Panama Refining Co. v. Ryan, 293 U.S. 388 (1935) (striking down a grant of what eight Justices viewed as unconfined discretion to decide whether or not to forbid interstate shipment of oil extracted in excess of

state-law quotas); A.L.A. Schechter Poultry Corp. v. United States, cited in n. 21 (unanimously invalidating essentially unlimited authority to promulgate "codes of fair competition" for various sectors of business and industry).

23. See Buttfield v. Stranahan, 192 U.S. 470 (1904); J. W. Hampton, Jr. & Co. v. United States, 276 U.S. 394 (1928).

24. Lichter v. United States, 334 U.S. 742 (1948).

25. 272 U.S. 52 (1926).

26. 295 U.S. 602 (1935).

27. 487 U.S. 654.

28. Crowell v. Benson, 285 U.S. 22 (1932). This conclusion too was unnecessary to the decision, since the Court set aside the challenged order on narrower grounds.

29. See 5 U.S.C. § 706 (Administrative Procedure Act), requiring judicial deference to agency decisions unless "arbitrary, capricious, or an abuse of discretion" or "[un]supported by substantial evidence" in cases required to be decided on the record after agency hearing.

30. See also Currie, Bankruptcy Judges and the Independent Judiciary, 16 Creighton L. Rev. 441 (1983).

31. See chap. 1.

32. National Cable Television Association v. United States, 415 U.S. 336 (1974).

33. Immigration and Naturalization Service v. Chadha, 462 U.S. 919 (1983).

34. Buckley v. Valeo, 424 U.S. 1 (1976); Bowsher v. Synar, 478 U.S. 714 (1986). On the appointment question see art. II, § 2: "The *President* . . . shall nominate, and by the advice and consent of the Senate, shall appoint . . . officers of the United States . . . ." The same section authorizes Congress to vest the power to appoint inferior officers "in the President alone, in the courts of law, or in the heads of departments," but not in itself.

35. Northern Pipeline Construction Co. v. Marathon Pipeline Co., 458 U.S. 50 (1982).

36. Clinton v. City of New York, 524 U.S. 417 (1998). See n. 20 of chap. 1.

CHAPTER FIVE

1. Murray's Lessee v. Hoboken Land & Improvement Co., 59 U.S. 272 (1856).

2. See, e.g., Hurtado v. California, 110 U.S. 516 (1880) (due process does

not embody the common-law right to indictment by a grand jury); Powell v. Alabama, 287 U.S. 45 (1932) (due process entitles an indigent defendant to counsel at state expense although the common law did not).

3. See, e.g., Duncan v. Louisiana, 391 U.S. 145 (1968).

4. See Davidson v. New Orleans, 96 U.S. 97 (1878) (notice and hearing); Tumey v. Ohio, 273 U.S. 510 (1927) (biased judge); Moore v. Dempsey, 261 U.S. 86 (1923) (mob-dominated trial); In re Winship, 397 U.S. 358 (1970) (proof beyond reasonable doubt); Brown v. Mississippi, 297 U.S. 278 (1936) (coerced confession); Mooney v. Holohan, 294 U.S. 103 (1935) (knowing use of perjured testimony).

5. See Mapp v. Ohio, 367 U.S. 643 (1961) (search and seizure); Malloy v. Hogan, 378 U.S. 1 (1964) (self-incrimination); Benton v. Maryland, 395 U.S. 784 (1969) (double jeopardy); Duncan v. Louisiana, 391 U.S. 145 (1968) (jury trial); Pointer v. Texas, 380 U.S. 400 (1965) (confrontation); Gideon v. Wainwright, 372 U.S. 335 (1963) (right to counsel); Furman v. Georgia, 408 U.S. 238 (1972) (cruel and unusual punishment). In the *Furman* case the Court held a particular death-penalty statute unconstitutional. Partly for historical reasons, however, the majority of the Justices have not been prepared to hold the death penalty itself inherently "cruel and unusual."

6. See W. LaFave & J. Israel, Criminal Procedure 767 (1985): "The assumption is that the system can function only if a high percentage of cases are disposed of by guilty plea and that this will happen only if concessions are granted to induce pleas." For criticism see Alschuler, The Changing Plea-Bargaining Debate, 69 Cal. L. Rev. 652 (1981); Langbein, Torture and Plea Bargaining, 46 U. Chi. L. Rev. 3 (1978); Langbein, Land Without Plea Bargaining: How the Germans Do It, 78 Mich. L. Rev. 204 (1979) (showing that the process is not inevitable).

7. Brady v. United States, 397 U.S. 742 (1970); Bordenkircher v. Hayes, 434 U.S. 357 (1978).

8. See the "Substantive Due Process" section of this chapter.

9. Earlier decisions had denied that such "privileges" qualified as "property." See, e.g., Bailey v. Richardson, 182 F.2d 46 (D.C. Cir. 1950).

10. See Goldberg v. Kelly, 397 U.S. 254 (1970); Board of Regents v. Roth, 408 U.S. 564 (1972).

11. See Mathews v. Eldridge, 425 U.S. 319 (1976).

12. See n. 10.

13. 419 U.S. 565 (1975).

14. Bi-Metallic Investment Co. v. State Board of Equalization, 239 U.S. 441 (1915); United States v. Florida East Coast Ry., 410 U.S. 224 (1973).

Statutes, however, commonly give the interested public the right to participate in general rulemaking proceedings at least by submitting written com-
ments. See, e.g., 5 U.S.C. § 553 (Administrative Procedure Act).

15. Home Ins. Co. v. Dick, 281 U.S. 397 (1930); Phillips Petroleum Co.
v. Shutts, 105 S. Ct. 2965 (1985). See generally B. Currie, Selected Essays
on the Conflict of Laws, chap. 5 (1963).

16. See, e.g., Union Refrigerator Transit Co. v. Kentucky, 199 U.S. 194
(1905) (extraterritorial taxation); International Shoe Co. v. Washington, 326
U.S. 310 (1945) (requiring "minimum contacts" between the controversy
and the state in whose courts it is decided in order to assure "fair play and
substantial justice"); World-Wide Volkswagen Corp. v. Woodson, 444 U.S.
286 (1980) (stressing due process limitations on state-court jurisdiction as
"instrument of interstate federalism").

17. 198 U.S. 45 (1905).

18. 410 U.S. 113 (1973). The only exception was to save the life of the
mother.

19. See the dissenting opinions of Justices Harlan and Holmes in *Lochner*
and of Justices White and Rehnquist in *Roe*, the latter insisting that the measure bore a "rational relation to a valid state objective." Compare the test for
the validity of federal laws under the Necessary and Proper Clause enunciated in McCulloch v. Maryland, discussed in chap. 3, which requires appropriate means to achieve legitimate ends.

20. Holden v. Hardy, 169 U.S. 366 (1898).

21. Bunting v. Oregon, 243 U.S. 426.

22. West Coast Hotel Co. v. Parrish, 300 U.S. 379.

23. See, e.g., United States v. Carolene Products Co., 304 U.S. 144
(1938) (upholding a plainly protectionist ban on the shipment of skimmed
milk fortified with coconut oil); Williamson v. Lee Optical Co., 348 U.S.
483 (1955) (upholding a featherbedding provision forbidding the fitting of
existing eyeglass lenses into new frames without a doctor's prescription).

24. Ferguson v. Skrupa, 372 U.S. 726. But see BMW of North America
v. Gore, 517 U.S. 559 (1996) (holding that an excessive award of punitive
damages for the sale of an automobile with minor paint damage offended the
Due Process Clause).

25. See Barron v. Baltimore, discussed in chap. 1.

26. See Stromberg v. California, 283 U.S. 359 (1931) (speech); Near v.
Minnesota, 283 U.S. 697 (1931) (press); De Jonge v. Oregon, 299 U.S. 353
(1937) (assembly); Cantwell v. Connecticut, 310 U.S. 353 (1940) (religion).
Cf. Hurtado v. California, discussed in the "Procedural Requirements"

section of this chapter, concluding that "due process" required only those *procedural* protections which were "fundamental" before a person could be deprived of "liberty."

27. West Virginia Board of Education v. Barnette, 319 U.S. 625 (1943).

28. Ibid.

29. See United States v. Carolene Products Co., 304 U.S. 144, 152–53 n.4 (1938). The same footnote suggested the Court would give similarly strict scrutiny to measures that impeded the political process or disadvantaged "discrete and insular minorities." This pronunciamento proved as clairvoyant as it was difficult to justify in terms of the words, history, or purposes of the Constitution.

30. See Shattuck, The True Meaning of the Term "Liberty" in those Clauses of the Federal and State Constitutions which Protect "Life, Liberty, and Property," 4 Harv. L. Rev. 365 (1891).

31. Allgeyer v. Louisiana, 165 U.S. 578 (1897).

32. Historically the term "process" referred sometimes to procedure in general and sometimes to the summons giving notice of legal proceedings. See Easterbrook, Substance and Due Process, 1982 Supreme Court Review 85.

33. J. Story, Commentaries on the Constitution of the United States § 1783.

34. Murray's Lessee v. Hoboken Land & Improvement Co., 59 U.S. 272 (1856); Davidson v. New Orleans, 96 U.S. 97 (1878).

35. Youngstown Sheet & Tube Co. v. Sawyer, cited in chap. 4 (Jackson, J., concurring). For the development of this idea in nineteenth-century Europe see C. Schmitt, Verfassungslehre 130–31, 147–50 (1928).

36. Mayo v. Wilson, 1 N.H. 53 (1817). See also Corwin, the Doctrine of Due Process of Law Before the Civil War, 24 Harv. L. Rev. 366 (1911).

37. Planned Parenthood v. Casey, 505 U.S. 833.

38. Maher v. Roe, 432 U.S. 464 (1977); Harris v. McRae, 448 U.S. 297 (1980). See also DeShaney v. Winnebago County Dept. of Social Services, 489 U.S. 189 (1989) (holding that the state had no constitutional duty to protect a child from his father).

39. The question nevertheless is not susceptible of a categorical answer in light of the decisions. See, for example, Truax v. Corrigan, 257 U.S. 312 (1921) (holding that a state could not abolish injunctive remedies for labor picketing); Currie, Positive and Negative Constitutional Rights, 53 U. Chi. L. Rev. 864 (1986).

40. Calder v. Bull, 3 U.S. 386 (1798).

41. Slaughter-House Cases, 83 U.S. 36 (1873) (Bradley, J., dissenting).

42. See Cong. Globe, 39th Cong., 1st Sess. 2786 (Senator Howard).

43. See, e.g., Adamson v. California, 332 U.S. 46, 71–72 (Black, J., dissenting).

44. See Conner v. Elliott, 59 U.S. 591, 594 (1856). As the Court acknowledged in the Slaughter-House Cases, the "sole purpose" of this provision "was to declare to the several States, that whatever those rights, as you grant or establish them to your own citizens, or as you limit or qualify, or impose restrictions on their exercise, the same, neither more nor less, shall be the measure of the rights of citizens of other States within your jurisdiction."

45. What article IV "did for the protection of citizens of one State against hostile and discriminating legislation of other States," Justice Stephen Field argued in dissent in the Slaughter-House Cases, "the fourteenth amendment does for the protection of every citizen of the United States against hostile and discriminating legislation against him in favor of others, whether they reside in the same or in different States." The Equal Protection Clause (see chap. 6) serves this purpose today; but history lends credence to the textual implication that it was meant to require states to *protect* blacks equally against crimes perpetrated by third parties. The debates are summarized in Fairman, Does the Fourteenth Amendment Incorporate the Bill of Rights?, 2 Stan. L. Rev. 5 (1949).

46. See The Federalist, no. 84 (Hamilton); 1 Annals of Congress 456 (1789) (Madison); Caplan, The History and Meaning of the Ninth Amendment, 69 Va. L. Rev. 223 (1983).

47. Roe v. Wade, cited in n. 18 (concurring opinion).

48. Scott v. Sandford, 60 U.S. 393 (1857).

49. Bowers v. Hardwick, 478 U.S. 186 (1986).

CHAPTER SIX

1. See Slaughter-House Cases, 83 U.S. 36 (1873).

2. See chap. 5.

3. See Slaughter-House Cases, discussed in chap. 5.

4. Strauder v. West Virginia, 100 U.S. 303 (1880).

5. 163 U.S. 537 (1896). See also Pace v. Alabama, 106 U.S. 583 (1883) (upholding a statute authorizing more severe penalties for unlawful sexual relations when the parties were of different races because blacks and whites were subject to equal sanctions).

6. Missouri ex rel. Gaines v. Canada, 305 U.S. 337 (1938).

7. 347 U.S. 483 (1954).

8. See D. Currie, The Constitution in the Supreme Court: The Second Century, 1888–1986 381 (1990).

9. Loving v. Virginia, 388 U.S. 1 (1967).

10. Shelley v. Kraemer, 334 U.S. 1 (1948).

11. See Bickel, The Original Understanding and the Segregation Decision, 69 Harv. L. Rev. 1 (1955).

12. Strauder v. West Virginia, cited in n. 4.

13. 438 U.S. 265 (1978).

14. Fullilove v. Klutznick, 448 U.S. 448 (1980).

15. See the discussion of nonracial classifications below.

16. Korematsu v. United States, 323 U.S. 214 (1944).

17. One may add that well-intentioned racial classifications tend to confirm undesirable racial stereotypes, depreciate the actual accomplishments of members of the favored group, and engender resentments against those who are preferred. See generally Regents of the University of California v. Bakke, cited in n. 13 (Powell, J., concurring).

18. 488 U.S. 469.

19. 515 U.S. 200.

20. Washington v. Davis, 426 U.S. 229 (1976).

21. See also the discussion of affirmative government duties in connection with the Due Process Clauses in chap. 5.

22. See the Slaughter-House Cases and Strauder v. Virginia, above.

23. Massachusetts Board of Retirement v. Murgia, 427 U.S. 307 (1976).

24. See Washington v. Davis, cited in n. 20.

25. See Palmore v. Sidoti, 466 U.S. 429 (1984) (emphasis added).

26. 377 U.S. 533 (1964). See also the discussion of Harper v. Virginia Board of Elections in the last section of this chapter.

27. United States v. Virginia, 518 U.S. 515 (1996).

28. Craig v. Boren, 453 U.S. 57 (1981).

29. Rostker v. Goldberg, 453 U.S. 57 (1981). Varying degrees of heightened scrutiny have also been employed from time to time to invalidate distinctions disadvantaging aliens (e.g., Graham v. Richardson, 403 U.S. 365 (1971)) or illegitimate children (Levy v. Louisiana, 391 U.S. 68 (1968)). Romer v. Evans, 517 U.S. 620 (1996), which struck down a state constitutional provision denying homosexuals legal protection against discrimination on the ground that it lacked a "rational relationship to a legitimate governmental purpose," may portend similarly heightened scrutiny for classifications based on sexual orientation.

30. "Equality of rights under the law shall not be denied or abridged by the United States or by any State on account of sex."

31. See, e.g., Strauder v. West Virginia, cited in n. 4.

32. Neal v. Delaware, 103 U.S. 370 (1881).

33. Yick Wo v. Hopkins, 118 U.S. 356 (1886).

34. The only exceptions are the Thirteenth Amendment, which forbids slavery whether private or public, and the Eighteenth, which forbade the private production or transportation of alcoholic beverages during the few years before it was repealed by the Twenty-first.

35. 109 U.S. 3.

36. See Katzenbach v. McClung, cited in chap. 3 (Commerce Clause); Jones v. Alfred H. Mayer Co., 392 U.S. 409 (1968) (giving an unexpectedly broad interpretation to Congress's authority to enforce the Thirteenth Amendment's prohibition of "slavery").

37. 334 U.S. 1 (1948).

38. Moose Lodge v. Irvis, 407 U.S. 163 (1972).

39. Burton v. Wilmington Parking Authority, 365 U.S. 715 (1962).

40. See also the decisions discussed in the last section of this chapter.

41. Bolling v. Sharpe, 347 U.S. 497 (1954).

42. See chap. 5.

43. Against this it may be argued that the Court had already held, despite a parallel argument, that the Due Process Clause of the Fourteenth Amendment made applicable to the states some of the limitations that the first eight Amendments had placed, in addition to due process, on the United States. See, e.g., Gideon v. Wainwright, noted in chap. 5 (Sixth Amendment right to counsel).

44. See the discussion in chap. 5.

45. See Amendment 14, § 2; D. Currie, The Constitution in the Supreme Court: The First Hundred Years 384 (1985).

46. Guinn v. United States, 238 U.S. 347 (1915). Even this decision did not put an end to effective circumvention of the amendment through grandfather clauses, for the state next exempted from generally applicable voting qualifications those who had been entitled to vote under the grandfather clause invalidated in *Guinn.* Another twenty years passed before the Court had the opportunity to declare this provision unconstitutional too. See Lane v. Wilson, 307 U.S. 268 (1939).

47. Nixon v. Herndon, 273 U.S. 536 (1927). See also Nixon v. Condon, 286 U.S. 73 (1932) (holding the state responsible for the decision of a party committee to exclude blacks, on the ground that state law giving authority to the committee rather than party membership made the committee the state's agent). Actually the explicit denials by advocates of the Equal Protection Clause that it applied to voting rights (see above) made the Fifteenth

Amendment, as the Court later recognized, a more plausible basis for these decisions than the Fourteenth. See United States v. Classic, 313 U.S. 299 (1941).

48. Grovey v. Townsend, 295 U.S. 45 (1935). See the "State Action" section of this chapter.

49. Marsh v. Alabama, 326 U.S. 501 (1946), protecting the right to distribute religious literature on the streets of the company town.

50. Smith v. Allwright, 321 U.S. 649 (1944); Terry v. Adams, 345 U.S. 461 (1953).

51. Harper v. Virginia Board of Elections, 383 U.S. 663 (1966). The Twenty-fourth Amendment, adopted two years before this decision, had already forbidden denial of the right to vote "by reason of failure to pay any poll tax or other tax," but only in *federal* elections.

52. Lassiter v. Northampton Election Board, 360 U.S. 45 (1959).

53. Oregon v. Mitchell, 400 U.S. 112 (1970). Section 2 of the Fifteenth Amendment authorizes Congress "to enforce this Article by appropriate legislation."

54. South Carolina v. Katzenbach, 383 U.S. 301.

CHAPTER SEVEN

1. See chap. 5.

2. Whitney v. California, 274 U.S. 357 (concurring opinion).

3. Schenck v. United States, 249 U.S. 47 (1919). It is somewhat more plausible to argue that the intention was to leave the entire subject of regulating communication to the *states*, since originally the First Amendment applied only to Congress. Even this interpretation would require holding the amendment inapplicable to the District of Columbia, where Congress has exclusive legislative authority; and it does not account for the explicit power of Congress to limit speech under the express power to enact copyright laws, art. I, § 8.

4. See 4 W. Blackstone, Commentaries on the Laws of England 151 (1765); L. Levy, Freedom of Speech and Press in Early American History: Legacy of Suppression (1960).

5. See, e.g., Near v. Minnesota, 283 U.S. 697 (1937); New York Times Co. v. United States, 403 U.S. 713 (1971).

6. Patterson v. Colorado, 205 U.S. 454 (1907).

7. See Near v. Minnesota, cited in n. 5.

8. T. Cooley, Constitutional Limitations 421 (1868). See also E. Freund, The Police Power §§ 474–75 (1904). Jeffersonians had made the same point

in opposing the infamous Sedition Act in 1798. See D. Currie, The Constitution in Congress: The Federalist Period, 1789–1801 260–62 (1997).

9. See chaps. 5 and 6.

10. See, e.g., NAACP v. Alabama, 357 U.S. 449 (1958) (freedom of association). Cf. chaps. 5 and 6.

11. 249 U.S. 47.

12. Holmes later added that the danger must be serious as well as clear and present. See Abrams v. United States, 250 U.S. 616 (1919) (dissenting opinion).

13. 341 U.S. 494.

14. Debs v. United States, 249 U.S. 211 (1919).

15. Justice Holmes recognized this in a later dissenting opinion: "A patriot might think that we were wasting money on aeroplanes, or making more cannon of a certain kind than we needed, and might advocate curtailment with success, yet even if it turned out that the curtailment hindered and was thought by other minds to have been obviously likely to hinder the United States in the prosecution of the war, no one would hold such conduct a crime." Abrams v. United States, 250 U.S. 616 (1919) (Holmes, J., dissenting).

16. 395 U.S. 444 (1969).

17. Village of Skokie v. National Socialist Party of America, 69 Ill.2d 890, 373 N.E.2d 21 (Illinois Supreme Court).

18. Whitney v. California, 274 U.S. 357 (1927) (concurring opinion).

19. New York Times Co. v. Sullivan, 376 U.S. 254 (1964).

20. NAACP v. Alabama, 357 U.S. 449 (1958). Three years later, despite a similar indirect threat to freedom of association, a divided Court questionably found a compelling ground of national security for requiring a list of members of the Communist Party. Communist Party v. Subversive Activities Board, 367 U.S. 1 (1961). No such justification was found, however, in a later case involving the Socialist Workers Party. Brown v. Socialist Workers '74 Campaign Committee, 459 U.S. 87 (1982).

21. Compare, e.g., Barenblatt v. United States, 360 U.S. 109 (1959), with DeGregory v. New Hampshire, 383 U.S. 825 (1966).

22. 427 U.S. 347 (1976).

23. See Joseph Burstyn, Inc. v. Wilson, 343 U.S. 495, 501 (1952); Winters v. New York, 333 U.S. 507, 501 (1948).

24. See Roth v. United States, 354 U.S. 476 (1957); Miller v. California, 413 U.S. 15 (1973). Recent ordinances punishing as "pornography" the "graphic sexually explicit subordination of women," however, cannot be defended on this ground, for their express aim is to suppress an idea: "The

Constitution forbids the state to declare one perspective right and silence opponents." American Booksellers Ass'n v. Hudnut, 771 F.2d 323 (7th Cir. 1985), aff'd mem, 475 U.S. 1001 (1986).

25. Valentine v. Chrestensen, 316 U.S. 52 (1942).

26. Virginia Pharmacy Board v. Virginia Consumer Council, 425 U.S. 748.

27. Central Hudson Gas v. Public Service Comm'n, 447 U.S. 557 (1980); Board of Trustees v. Fox, 492 U.S. 469 (1989).

28. Cox v. Louisiana (I), 379 U.S. 536 (1965).

29. Kovacs v. Cooper, 336 U.S. 77 (1949).

30. International Society for Krishna Consciousness v. Lee, 505 U.S. 672 (1992).

31. United States v. O'Brien, 391 U.S. 367 (1968). With the benefit of hindsight, this argument does not appear particularly convincing.

32. Clark v. Community for Creative Non-Violence, 468 U.S. 288 (1984).

33. See United States v. O'Brien, cited in n. 31: "We cannot accept the view that an apparently limitless variety of conduct can be labeled 'speech' whenever the person engaging in the conduct intends thereby to express an idea."

34. Stromberg v. California, 283 U.S. 359 (1931).

35. Schneider v. State, 308 U.S. 147 (1939).

36. Cox v. Louisiana (I), 379 U.S. 536 (1965).

37. Compare Grayned v. City of Rockford, 408 U.S. 104 (1972).

38. Police Department v. Mosley, 408 U.S. 92 (1972).

39. Time, place, and manner regulations that discriminate according to content may also offend the Equal Protection Clause. See., e.g., Carey v. Brown, 447 U.S. 455 (1980); see also chap. 6.

40. As an indication of how seriously the Court takes the principle against viewpoint discrimination in time, place, and manner regulations see R. A. V. v. City of St. Paul, 505 U.S. 377 (1992), and United States v. Eichman, 496 U.S. 310 (1990), respectively striking down prohibitions of cross-burning and flag-burning because they discriminated according to the message the actor intended to convey.

41. It is not always easy to determine whether the government itself is speaking or whether it is subsidizing private speech. See, e.g., Rust v. Sullivan, 500 U.S. 173 (1991) (upholding a ban on abortion counseling in the context of programs receiving federal family-planning funds). Nobody suggests that if the government embarks on a war against drugs it must give equal time to dope peddlers; yet if the government itself emitted blatant partisan propaganda it would run afoul of the First Amendment.

42. Greer v. Spock, 424 U.S. 828 (1976).

43. Burson v. Freeman, 504 U.S. 191 (1992).

44. Cox v. Louisiana (I), 379 U.S. 536 (1965). Compare the general discussion of delegated powers in chap. 4.

CHAPTER EIGHT

1. See New York Times Co. v. United States, 403 U.S. 713 (1971) (federal court may not abridge freedom of the press).

2. Everson v. Board of Education, 330 U.S. 1 (1947). Compare the decisions applying freedom of expression to the states, noted in chaps. 5 and 7.

3. Compare Elrod v. Burns, noted in chap. 7, where the Court invalidated a similar indirect restriction of *political* freedom.

4. See n. 7.

5. Torcaso v. Watkins, 367 U.S. 488 (1961). State action discriminating on religious grounds would also offend the Equal Protection Clause in most instances (see chap. 6). Article VI expressly forbids the *United States* to prescribe "any religious test . . . as a qualification to any office or public trust . . . ."

6. Compare the discussion in chap. 7.

7. See the materials collected in A. Stokes & L. Pfeffer, Church and State in the United States (1964), and especially the quotation from Roger Williams at p. 15.

8. Reynolds v. United States, 98 U.S. 145.

9. Hamilton v. Regents, 293 U.S. 245 (1934) (military training); Braunfeld v. Brown, 366 U.S. 599 (1961) (Sunday law); Goldman v. Weinberger, 475 U.S. 503 (1986) (head covering). Today conscientious objectors are exempted from military service by *statute*, whether or not their objections are based upon a belief in God. See United States v. Seeger, 380 U.S. 163 (1965).

The same conception of neutrality underlay the controversial decision in Minersville School District v. Gobitis, 310 U.S. 586 (1940), that Jehovah's Witnesses enjoyed no exemption from a general requirement that school children salute the flag, although in their eyes the ceremony offended the Second Commandment. Only three years later the Court declared the flag-salute law unconstitutional on the persuasive ground that *no one* could be compelled to affirm unpalatable opinions in light of the guarantee of freedom of speech. West Virginia Board of Education v. Barnette, 319 U.S. 624 (1943).

10. 374 U.S. 398 (1963).

11. 406 U.S. 205 (1972).

12. 402 U.S. 872.

13. City of Boerne v. Flores, 521 U.S. 507 (1957). See Currie, RFRA, 39 Wm. & Mary L. Rev. 637 (1998).

14. See Everson v. Board of Education, cited in n. 2.

15. See Marsh v. Chambers, 463 U.S. 783 (1983); Terrett v. Taylor, 13 U.S. 43 (1815).

16. Everson v. Board of Education, cited in n. 2.

17. Engel v. Vitale, 370 U.S. 421 (1962); Abingdon School Dist. v. Schempp, 374 U.S. 203 (1963); Wallace v. Jaffree, 472 U.S. 38 (1985).

18. The Court had already held that a taxpayer could not show a sufficient pocketbook injury to entitle him to challenge Bible reading in the public schools. Doremus v. Board of Education, 342 U.S. 429 (1952).

19. The quotation, taken from Jefferson, was repeated in Everson v. Board of Education, n. 2 above. The Court's most recent pronouncement on this subject, however, conspicuously eschewed all references to state sponsorship of religion, relying instead upon the "coercive" effect of prayers at graduation ceremonies. Lee v. Weisman, 505 U.S. 577 (1992).

20. McGowan v. Maryland, 366 U.S. 420 (1961). Compare Washington v. Davis, discussed in chap. 6, where the Court refused to strike down a law serving a legitimate purpose as racially discriminatory under the Equal Protection Clause simply because it incidentally injured more blacks than whites.

21. Stone v. Graham, 449 U.S. 39 (1980).

22. Bradford v. Roberts, 175 U.S. 291 (1899).

23. Board of Education v. Allen, 392 U.S. 236 (1968).

24. Tilton v. Richardson, 403 U.S. 672 (1971); Roemer v. Maryland Public Works Board, 426 U.S. 736 (1976).

25. 403 U.S. 602.

26. 463 U.S. 388 (1983).

27. The governing test was stated in Lemon v. Kurtzman, cited in n. 25: "First, the statute must have a secular legislative purpose; second, its principal or primary effect must be one that neither advances nor inhibits religion . . . ; finally, the statute must not foster 'an excessive governmental entanglement with religion.'" The Court repeated this test in *Mueller*, though several Justices have since questioned its viability.

28. 330 U.S. 1 (1947).

29. Witters v. Washington Dept. of Services for the Blind, 474 U.S. 481 (1986).

30. 397 U.S. 664 (1970).

31. E.g., Rosenberger v. Rector and Visitors of the University of Virginia,

515 U.S. 819 (1995) (holding it unconstitutional to exclude religious periodicals from a general subsidy of student publications).

32. See P. Kurland, Religion and the Law (1962).

CHAPTER NINE

1. See chap. 3.

2. See chap. 6.

3. See, e.g., Ex parte McCardle, discussed in chap. 2, where one of several efforts to challenge the Reconstruction Act failed for want of jurisdiction; D. Currie, The Constitution in the Supreme Court: The First Hundred Years 296–376 (1985).

4. See, e.g., Debs v. United States, Dennis v. United States, and Barenblatt v. United States, discussed in chap. 7.

5. See chap. 4.

6. See chap. 6.

7. Dred Scott v. Sandford, noted in chap. 5.

8. E.g., Lochner v. New York, discussed in chap. 5.

9. See Roe v. Wade, also discussed in chap. 5.

10. The Federalist, no. 78.

11. Ex parte Milligan, 71 U.S. 2 (1866); Cummings v. Missouri, 71 U.S. 277 (1867); Ex parte Garland, 71 U.S. 333 (1867).

12. See chap. 5.

13. See chaps. 6 and 8; Reynolds v. Sims, 377 U.S. 533 (1964) (equal apportionment of legislative seats).

14. See chap. 7.

15. See H. L. A. Hart, The Concept of Law 138–41 (1961).

APPENDIX B

1. Proposed in 1789, this amendment was not ratified by three fourths of the states until 1992. Although both Congress and the executive proclaimed that the amendment had been adopted, doubts as to its validity persist because of the long delay between proposal and ultimate ratification.

BIBLIOGRAPHY

Commentary on the Constitution is quite voluminous. This bibliography mentions only a few of the more prominent books (as well as, of course, my own), omitting shorter pieces altogether.

BASIC SOURCE MATERIALS

Elliot, J. Debates in the Several State Conventions on the Adoption of the Federal Constitution (2d ed. 1836).
Farrand, M. The Records of the Federal Convention of 1787 (rev. ed. 1966).
The Federalist Papers (J. Cooke ed. 1961).
Kurland, P., and R. Lerner. The Founders' Constitution (1986).

HISTORIES

Bickel, A., and B. Schmidt. 9 History of the Supreme Court of the United States (1984).
Fairman, C. 6 and 7 History of the Supreme Court of the United States (1971, 1987).
Fiss, O. 8 History of the Supreme Court of the United States (1993).
Goebel, J. 1 History of the Supreme Court of the United States (1971).
Haines, C., and F. Sherwood. The Role of the Supreme Court in American Government and Politics (1944 and 1957).
Haskins, G., and H. Johnson. 2 History of the Supreme Court of the United States (1981).
Hyman, H., and W. Wiecek. Equal Justice Under Law: Constitutional Development, 1835–1875 (1982).
Kelly, A., and W. Harbison. The American Constitution: Its Origins and Development (7th ed. 1991).
McLaughlin, A. A Constitutional History of the United States (1935).
Murphy, P. The Constitution in Crisis Times: 1918–1969 (1972).
Swisher, C. 5 History of the Supreme Court of the United States (1974).
Warren, C. The Supreme Court in United States History (rev. ed. 1926).
White, G. E. 3 History of the Supreme Court of the United States (1991).
Wright, B. The Growth of American Constitutional Law (1942).

Biographies

Beveridge, A. The Life of John Marshall (1919).
Biddle, F. Mr. Justice Holmes (1942).
Dunne, G. Joseph Story and the Rise of the Supreme Court (1970).
Dunne, G. Hugo Black and the Judicial Revolution (1977).
Fairman, C. Mr. Justice Miller and the Supreme Court (1939).
Hutchinson, D. The Man Who Once Was Whizzer White (1998).
Kaufman, A. Cardozo (1998).
King, W. Melville Weston Fuller (1950).
Latham, F. The Great Dissenter: John Marshall Harlan (1970).
Magrath, C. Morrison R. Waite: The Triumph of Character (1963).
Mason, A. Brandeis: A Free Man's Life (1946).
Mason, A. Harlan Fiske Stone: Pillar of the Law (1956).
Mason, A. William Howard Taft: Chief Justice (1964).
Novick, S. Honorable Justice: The Life of Oliver Wendell Holmes (1989).
Paschal, J. Mr. Justice Sutherland: A Man Against the State (1951).
Pusey, M. Charles Evans Hughes (1951).
Schwartz, B. Super Chief: Earl Warren and His Supreme Court (1983).
Swisher, C. Roger B. Taney (1936).
Swisher, C. Stephen J. Field, Craftsman of the Law (1930).
Thomas, H. Felix Frankfurter: Scholar on the Bench (1960).
White, G. E. Earl Warren: A Public Life (1982).
Yarbrough, T. Judicial Enigma: The First Justice Harlan (1995).

Treatises

Cooley, T. Constitutional Limitations (1868).
Nowak, J., R. Rotunda, and J. Young. Constitutional Law (5th ed. 1995).
Story, J. The Constitution of the United States (1833).
Tribe, L. American Constitutional Law (3d ed. 2000).

Casebooks

Gunther, G., and K. Sullivan. Constitutional Law (13th ed. 1997).
Stone, G., L. Seidman, C. Sunstein, and M. Tushnet. Constitutional Law (3d ed. 1996).

Other Works

Bickel, A. The Least Dangerous Branch (1962).
Chafee, Z. Free Speech in the United States (1941).

Choper, J. Judicial Review and the National Political Process (1980).

Corwin, E. Corwin on the Constitution (R. Loss ed. 1981).

Currie, D. The Constitution in the Supreme Court: The First Hundred Years (1985).

Currie, D. The Constitution in the Supreme Court: The Second Century (1990).

Currie, D. The Constitution in Congress: The Federalist Period, 1789–1801 (1997).

Currie, D. The Constitution in Congress: The Jeffersonians, 1801–1829 (forthcoming).

Ely, J. Democracy and Distrust (1980).

Farber, D. The First Amendment (1998).

Freund, P. The Supreme Court of the United States (1949).

Kalven, H. A Worthy Tradition: Freedom of Speech in America (1988).

Kurland, P. Religion and the Law (1962).

Kurland, P. Watergate and the Constitution (1978).

Meiklejohn, A. Free Speech and its Relation to Self-Government (1948).

McCloskey, R. The American Supreme Court (2d ed. 1994).

Powell, T. Vagaries and Varieties in Constitutional Litigation (1956).

INDEX